A Semi-Buddhist Ex-Comedian Golf Junkie

Finds Joy
in the
Kingdom of Thailand

MIKE NEUN

Publishing Partners

Publishing Partners
Port Townsend, WA
www.marciabreece.com
marcia@marciabreece.com

Library of Congress Control Number: 2020909659

ISBN: 978-1-944887-55-1
eBook ISBN: 978-1-944887-56-8

Interior layout: Marcia Breece
Cover design: Marcia Breece
eBook: Marcia Breece

Mike and Jintana

CONTENTS

A Semi-Buddhist Ex-Comedian Golf Junkie
Finds Joy in the Kingdom of Thailand

A Day in the Life

I am back from taking Jintana's niece, Awee, to school and meeting Jintana for breakfast. We live in Chiangmai, Thailand, and traffic was awful this morning. Worse than usual. I wonder how much longer I'll be capable of driving.

In my defense, I ask people if my driving sucks, because I don't want to be one of those dangerous old guys who doesn't know he's drifting from lane to lane and just missing families on motorbikes. I have no pride when it comes to driving, but I do love the freedom it gives me.

This morning Jintana's phone alarm went off at 5:30 a.m. and for once I was not awake beforehand. I can't remember the last time I had a full night's sleep, but my naps are awesome. Sometimes I get wild entertainment dreams. Yesterday's was this: I was on a terrible cruise ship with a show to do and someone had stolen my guitar and the cruise director had stolen my act and, oh yes, we were sinking. I retired 15 years ago. Shouldn't those dreams have gone away by now? My other reoccurring nightmare is going out in front of a huge crowd and the microphone turns into a hot dog and the guitar strings into spaghetti. Thousands of people are screaming, "We can't hear you!" and I'm yelling, "The microphone is a hot dog!"

I once mentioned these dreams to a dancer and she said she had dreams of going on stage and forgetting the routines. She'd be trying to follow the other dancers and screwing everything up. In another one, she would be about to go on stage and realize she'd forgotten her costume. The stage hands would push her out and she'd be dancing naked in Radio City Music Hall. I realized that visual would stay with me a long time.

Today I wake up and lie there for awhile. It's cold for Thailand, about 13 degrees Celsius, and my wife is bundled up, including socks and an extra blanket. It brings back memories of a long ago relationship when my loved one gradually began wearing more and more shapeless clothes to bed. Being highly intuitive, I realized she wasn't yearning for my body. Jintana is just cold and we're still good together.

I lie there musing on all the people sleeping with no one to hold or with someone who doesn't want to be held. I'm not sure which is worse.

Jintana gets up and goes to the bathroom to plug in the hot water pot. I'm trying cut down on coffee so I go out to the refrigerator in the upstairs hall and get some coffee-chocolate beans to nibble on while I drink hot water and watch YouTube. Kobe Bryant and his daughter have died in a helicopter crash. To me, she is the sadder part of the story. He had a good life, she was just starting. My feelings about him are mixed. He was a sensational basketball player, but I never thought of him as a good teammate. How would I know? I don't. I have no clue. And yes, he was charged with sexual assault and claimed it was consensual. He was let off when the 19-year-old woman refused to testify. Then there was a civil case that was settled with money, an apology to her and her family and no admission of guilt. Who knows what happened there? Some guys are horrible to women, some women are out to rip off big stars. I'm working from no facts whatsoever. I should get a podcast.

As my wife showers and gets ready for work at the university, I watch YouTube clips of car rebuilds, David Spade's new show, Australian Open tennis, bits from the Graham

Mike Neun

Norton Show, and other short-attention-span tidbits. Then I go to the bathroom, splash water on my face and hair, brush my teeth and get dressed for my driver duties. My job is to take Jintana's older niece, Kadjang, to Prince Royal Academy. It's a fine high school and very difficult to get into. Awee, Kadjang's younger sister, did not have good enough grades to get in next year and when she found out she was heartbroken. She dreamed of going to the same school as her sister, but now she'll go to a different one and that's probably okay. I think Kadjang is a better student and I also think they'll both do just fine in life. They are the best kids I've ever known. Jintana will drive Awee, the younger, to Wichai Wittayai junior high school and then meet me at Bake 'n Bite for breakfast.

Kadjang and I get in my old Nissan Almera, I start my Richard Russo audio book, and we head out for school. Kadjang sits in the back seat and does her hair. Thai people think seat belts are only to be used in the front seat. I have no idea why this is, but again I ask her to put one on and again she says she has to do her hair first. I open the electric gate, she checks for cars, and I back out. I drive up to the highway, turn left, and we are off. Fifteen minutes later I turn off the Super Highway toward town, traffic slows to a crawl and soon we are bumper to bumper on the road to her school. I listen to my book, she talks to friends on her phone, and I weave through the mass of cars to drop her off. She thanks me for driving, I say have a good day, and I try to pull out from the curb but a woman in a Toyota refuses to give an inch. I wait, and slowly, slowly, fight the traffic to get to Bake n' Bite. I'm late, and Jintana has to eat without me. I get there as she is leaving for work, say goodbye, and sit down to eat my spinach Quiche with very strong coffee. Cutting down might be harder than I thought.

I read the sports and news on my phone. More about Kobe. More about the Trump impeachment. I pick up quiche to go for Jintana's mom, and head back home.

Usually I stop at the Gymkhana driving range on the way home, but I've been going at golf pretty hard and my back is acting up. On the way I stop at RimPing Market across from the Ping River. I have a deep desire for Thin Mints, those chocolate wafers with a mint filling, and discover they don't have any. I accept a substitute, and see some dijon mustard Kettle potato chips. They call to me, and I find my self cheerfully smiling as I pick up a bag. I eat them on the way home—potato chips and quiche, breakfast of champions.

Now I am upstairs in our room, reclined in my recliner chair with the blow-up pillow behind the small of my back and my legs propped up on the bed. I decide to write a book. This is it.

HA! YOU? WRITE A BOOK?

I should define "book." My definition: 60,000 words. That's it. I don't care if it has characters, a plot, a beginning or an end. In short, none of that technical stuff authors waffle on about in seminars.

Also, I was a journalism major in college and know what a complete sentence is. I think they're overrated. You will find phrases here, standing alone, and I don't want some pedant blathering on about them. People don't talk in complete sentences and I don't write in them. Sue me.

My goal is to complete this. I have started writing lots of books and never come close to finishing. Mastery is hard. Completion might be doable so I'm setting the bar low. I will do this.

When I get home from breakfast this morning I realize I am extremely sleepy, so I lie down for a quick nap. That turns into three hours of deep sleep, much deeper than I'd had the night before. I spent 45 years on the road, sleeping in motels, hotels, casinos, and cruise ships. I can't remember when I ever had a complete night's sleep. In the early years, I had some pretty impressive pass outs, as liquor was a big part of my life, but even then I would wake up in the middle of the night, read, roll around, and eventually get back to sleep.

When I wake up from my nap, groggy, about 1:30 in the afternoon, I decide to get a light lunch and go hit golf balls. The light lunch idea goes out the window when I see Francesca's is open and Tony, the owner and head chef, recommends spaghetti bolognese. That and a cappuccino, plus time watching Netflix as I eat, just about puts me back to sleep. I watch the beginning of a documentary about the Ottoman Empire and again wonder how any thinking human being could come up with the concept of war. To me, it is the ultimate in stupidity and there is no glory whatsoever. Screams, blood, explosions, severed limbs and bullets zipping everywhere—who comes up with shit like that?

I eat my spaghetti, watch the beginning of the war for Constantinople, pay my 270 baht, about 8 bucks, and walk out to the Almera. I have about an hour to kill before picking up Awee at school, so I drive to Stardome driving range and ask for two trays of balls, 40 balls each. Ah, but there is a promotion and I get four trays for 100 baht, about three dollars. I know I can't hit that many but I figure I'll just give away the leftover balls.

I go back to a practicing technique that worked years ago when I could actually break 80 occasionally. I know this sounds pretty deep, but I discovered if I could get the bottom of my golf swing somewhere near the ball I could actually make contact. With most clubs, that place should be a couple of inches in front of the ball, so that you hit the ball, then the turf. You'd think a person could do that. Not me. So now I take a practice swing, trying to put the bottom of the swing ahead of the ball, then take a real swing to try to do the same. Two trays equals 80 practice swings and 80 real swings. I don't do full shots, because my back would fall apart, but I feel if I can make contact on a half swing, I can do it on a full one. I will give it a month and see if I can get back into the 70s.

The big question is why?

Mike Neun

I have no answer.

When I retired from my career in comedy I turned to my first love, golf, and thought if I practiced and played I would get better. Silly me. In my years on the road I'd managed to perfect a flawed swing that produced a lot of fat shots. Frustrating. Also it only took eight years to figure out I couldn't play afternoon golf in the Thai heat. Mad dogs, Englishmen and golf leagues in Chiangmai all go out in the midday sun and it's insane.

Enough about golf. I picked up Awee and headed home.

My wife just got home from work and I realize she'd asked me to strip the sheets and pillow cases off the bed this morning and I'd totally forgotten. So we do it now in silence, with the firm understanding that the bed should've been airing out all day. I am a failure at bed airing out.

My wife works hard. She has a full-time job as secretary to the dean of music at Payap University. She also keeps the house clean and does laundry, with the modest help of her two teen-age nieces. It's a big house, built by her family, and I have offered many times to pay for a maid to help her out. We had a maid when we first moved in. Bo was a girl from Mom's village up in the hills and she lived with us for a few years. She became part of the family and Jintana's family helped her get her citizenship card, which is a big deal in Thailand. Then she fell in love with a guy from the village, moved back and got married.

Jintana doesn't want a new maid. She doesn't want a stranger in her house, so she does the housework.

My contribution is to drive kids to school and various activities. I also do my own ironing, as I spent 45 years on the road. Heck, I can steam out a suit with a travel iron. I have skills! I offered to do my own laundry but she doesn't trust me with the washing machine. I have also tried to help clean house, but gave up when I vacuumed the whole upstairs only to find her re-vacuuming 20 minutes later. Either she thinks I'm totally inept, or Thai people have a very firm idea of women's work and men's work. I think it's the latter. I also share the money I made doing comedy for 45 years. I like the idea of helping pay for the kids' schools, meals in restaurants, and stuff around the house.

The bed is made. It's twilight. I have nothing to do this evening because I've decided to take a month off from people. I've always been kind of a loner, with interludes where I try to be sociable. That was a lot easier years ago when I was drinking.

Later on I watch the documentary, "Senna", about Arton Senna, the race driver who died in a crash at age 34. I am sad. I think about all the things we try to do in life, and how inconsequential they become in the end. I think of Kobe Bryant, Senna, and the unknowns who never achieve greatness but try hard to do well and realize in the end it's not a big deal. I was going to become a great entertainer, a master of music and comedy, and maybe, on a few nights, I achieved it. I know now I didn't work hard enough, or smart enough. Senna and Kobe did, and both died young. I guess it matters, but I also think the joy is in the process, not the results or the legacy.

So now I sit in the bedroom, my wife across from me watching something on Netflix. She is a good woman, and the past 13 years with her have been the best of my life. We live quietly. I try to be a good husband, but I think I'm difficult to live with. My first two marriages failed and other relationships did too. Maybe now that I'm not on the road and obsessed with work I'm easier to live with. I hope so.

Mike Neun

DICTATORS AND
OTHER CRAZY PEOPLE

I wake up at 4:30 a.m. and realize I have almost an hour before I have to get up for an early round of golf. For once, I'm able to go back to sleep and the alarm wakes me at 5:20. I remember waking up around 2 a.m. and listening to a lecture on stoicism on YouTube for awhile before I could get back to sleep. Stoicism seems related to Buddhism, so now they both fascinate me, as does Marcus Arelius, the Roman emperor who had absolute power and could've wallowed in corruption and pleasure. Instead he spent years trying to become a good person.

Someone should come up with a ratio of bad dictators to good, but my feeling is the chances of getting a good dictator are about one percent. Yet people still fall for strongman leaders. Putin, Erdogan, Duterte, Xi Jinping, and all the other autocrats—people actually think that's a good way to go. Now, Trump. He fits the pattern and it scares me.

But I digress, and I get the feeling there will be more digressions in this book than actual action. I can do that because I'm a strongman author. I make my own rules.

I wake up in darkness. And again it's cold. For Thailand this is the dead of winter and the early temperature today is

15 degrees. I have no idea what that is in Fahrenheit, but I think it would be a mildly cold day in Seattle. Here it's Arctic.

I splash water on my hair and face (I showered before going to bed and don't think I got dirty sleeping), plug in the hot water pot and get dressed. Shorts, golf shirt, sweatshirt, another sweatshirt, and I'm ready. A little before six I head downstairs, turn off the outside lights, put on socks and my favorite Adidas shoes (wide, very wide) and head out to the car. I plug my phone into the dash and put on the Richard Russo novel. He wrote "Nobody's Fool", one of my all-time favorite books and one of my all-time favorite Paul Newman movies. I'm now going through all his books and they're amazing.

It takes less than ten minutes to get to North Hill golf course and there I meet Jeff, the guy who has a coffee-roasting business in Kelowna, British Columbia.

Jeff is one of the Canadian contingent I've met in Chiangmai, starting with Derek Schade, the golf pro who used to be at Chiangmai Highlands and is one of my favorite people in Thailand. His friend Jeff loves early, fast golf, so we are perfectly suited to play together. Oh sure, he outdrives me by about 100 yards and has me leaping out of my shoes trying for extra distance, but he is positive, good to talk to, and a new friend.

We pay our green fees, 1200 baht (about 40 bucks) for me with my membership and 1600 for his guest fees. Both include golf carts and caddies.

Okay, time to talk about Thailand golf, and caddies in particular. Almost all Thai caddies are women and it is a decent-paying job. Not great, but certainly a step up from working in rice fields, standing behind a counter in some shop, or cleaning houses. The caddies are generally fairly young, cheerful, good at their jobs, and they add a huge amount to the game. If you find a good caddy, you can book her for all your rounds. I had a great caddy at Chiangmai Highlands, Aura, and she worked with me for 12 years until my membership ran out and I couldn't afford a new one. When she first started caddying for me I played with a group called The Royal League that teed off at noon. That's right, I joined a group that thought teeing off at the absolute peak of Thai heat was a really good idea. They liked it because they could transition right from golf to drinking beer. Nothing like an overly competitive round—you'd think we were playing the National Open—under a blazing sun to bring out the worst in all of us.

Aura in the beginning was quiet and shy, and kind of scared of The Royal League because the golfers yelled a lot. We had big arguments about rules infractions and handicaps to the point where one night the leader of the league walked out of a bar in Chiangmai and was attacked by one of his golfers. Yes, the gentlemen's game.

After playing in that league I finally got out and discovered my quiet, timid caddy had a wonderful sense of humor and was a strong woman. We called each other "Boss." She is still one of the best people I've met in Thailand.

At North Hill, where I now play, I got lucky and found Ploy, who is also excellent and has a better golf swing than I do. I was playing alone one day with her caddying and I was feeling pretty good about my game. Then we had a free moment and she swung my driver. Awesome!

I like to think I have more empathy for the caddies because I caddied a bit when I was in high school. I wasn't great. I wore thick glasses and didn't see the ball, so I had to hope my golfers knew where it went. My worst loop (18 holes was a "loop", caddies were "loopers") was carrying two bags on a hot day, when one golfer sliced and the other hooked. I spent four hours running back and forth across the fairways and on the last hole, an uphill par 5, the smallest caddy out there had to help me get those bags up the hill.

Jeff and I pay our fees and head out in the dark to meet the caddies. We are on the tee at 6:15 and it's still pitch black. About 6:25, two Japanese guys, walking, drift up to the tee and we realize we have to tee off if we want to go first and not be held up by slow play. The caddies use their phone flashlights to try to see the ball and we tee off in the dark. The phone flashlights are useless and nobody sees the balls but mine feels left, Jeff thinks his is down the middle. We find mine in the right rough, not even close to where I thought it would be, and can't find Jeff's at all. I'm guessing it wasn't down the middle.

On this first hole, a par five, (don't worry, I'm not going to give a boring play-by-play of the round) I've been hitting two decent shots and then chunking my approach shot. Today I varied it by chunking my second shot. Oh well. We're off.

By the second hole we can see, and Jeff and I play a wonderful round. We have the course to ourselves, we have cool (okay, maybe cold) weather, and both of us love to play fast. North Hill has lots of water, and we both dunk some balls, but we also hit some good shots. The greens are lightning fast so there are some three-putts involved. We play our 18 holes in under 2 1/2 hours, head to the car, tip the caddies, and I drive us to the Bagel House for breakfast. Yes, Chiangmai has a Bagel House where you have a choice of different bagels and good breakfasts. Oh sure, maybe not traditional Thai food but the city now has restaurants of all kinds.

By 10:30 I'm back home, in bed, zonked out for my morning nap. Again I realize I now sleep better in the daytime than I do at night. I'm not sure that's a good thing.

The coronavirus is sweeping through China and there are cases reported in Chiangmai. Not surprising, as we have many Chinese tourists here. I plan to stay out of downtown as much as possible. Everyone is wearing masks, but I doubt

Mike Neun

if they do very much to protect people. The masks are simple and normally used to protect from massive pollution during rice field burning season, which is just beginning. I wear the mask sometimes because my wife wants me to, but I feel smothered and don't like it.

It's later in the day and I just got back from taking my passport into the visa service, where they will take care of the 90-day address notification at Thai immigration. We foreigners have to get this done every three months and then renew our visas once a year. I used to do it myself, but each visit took a day out of my life and that seemed silly. So now I pay a visa service to do it for me.

Thai immigration is now making some foreigners get health insurance, but luckily my visa isn't included. Can you imagine an 80-year-old guy with residual prostate cancer walking into a health insurance company? They would fall down laughing. The words, "pre-existing condition" would ring through the halls. The good news is health care here is quite good (I have a fine oncologist who has kept me alive long past my sell date) and inexpensive.

Jeff told me today that if you drive to Vancouver, B.C., and register at a downtown hotel, you get charged 70 dollars per night to park your car. For the price of parking your car you can get a two-night's stay at a quite good hotel in Chiangmai with free parking. I choose Thailand.

So I drive to town, drop off my visa and go to Butter is Better, our other favorite breakfast restaurant for a snack. When I get there they tell me they've run out of food! That has never happened before and it takes me awhile to grasp that I couldn't get granola, fruit and yogurt, the meal I'd pictured on the way over. So I drive back out of town and go to Danisa's for a falafel wrap and latte. To be clear, I love Thai food and eat it all the time, I just wasn't in the mood this particular day. I'd thought about calling my old bridge partner to see if he wanted lunch, but then I realized he never calls me so screw it. Then I realized I'd broken up our partnership because I'd felt we were in a rut, so he could be a bit bitter. I would be if I were him but then, being a wonderfully forgiving guy, I would call. Yeah, right.

Instead, I eat and watch a video about Marshawn Lynch, a football player who grew up in the projects in Oakland and is known as "Beast Mode." If you want to picture my all-time exact athletic opposite, Beast Mode would be the guy. He is big, fast, scary, and loves crashing into people. Enough said.

I'm now back home. Jintana and the kids should be home soon. I have no plans. If my back feels all right I might go hit some balls and work on my getting-the-bottom-of-the-swing-in-the-right-place techniques. I think that's the most dashes I've ever used in a sentence.

COMEDIAN LOSES MIND, FINDS IT

Spokane, Washington, sometime in the 1970's:

In my career I did seven one-man shows for KSPS public television in Spokane. They were shown nationally on PBS and I was really happy with them. I think five of them were done at The Met Theater, which was a wonderful old theater, perfect for me. I would spend a year putting together a 90-minute show and they would tape it, edit out the best hour, and put it on the network.

If you realize a good joke can take just a few seconds and I was filling up an hour and a half, you can understand the pressure of writing this much material in a year. I did most of the work in my car, driving around and rehearsing the show to myself, adding bits and pieces as I drove. Then I'd try out the new stuff when I worked clubs and colleges. The TV shows did well and I kept getting asked to do new ones.

But on this morning, the day of the show, I woke up and couldn't remember one word of the material I was going to perform that night. Not one word. It was a total blank. I got out of bed, dressed, left the hotel, and walked around

Spokane hoping the mental block would leave and the show would return. It didn't. I'd had mental problems before, mostly in the form of panic attacks where everything would go out of kilter and I'd be afraid I was going crazy. The term, "panic attack", wasn't even in the conversation back then and I figured I was on the short list for the looney bin. This morning was worse because the attack lasted all that time I was walking around, an empty space in my brain where a year's work was supposed to be.

Finally I went back to the hotel and climbed into bed. I slept. When I awoke the show was back. Apparently it had decided to take a vacation. I went on stage that night and all went well, but I never trusted my mind again.

It is 10:30 a.m. in Chiangmai and I have delivered Kadjang to school, met Jintana for breakfast at Butter is Better, and gone to M-Sport driving range, again trying to get the bottom of the swing where I wanted it. How hard can this be I thought as I hit half my shots fat. Luckily I'm filled with inner peace and it didn't piss me off. Okay, there might've been swear words involved. After about 60 soft, short swings, my back started acting up. When this happens I get a really sharp pain in the lower right of my back, and it can get to the point where I'm afraid to move. Today, I walked down to the end of the range and laid down on one of the mats. I laid on my back and let things settle, then did some small crunches, keeping my lower back firm on the mat. After about 15 minutes I got up and the pain was gone. I went back to hit more balls and all was well.

As far as the swing goes, I feel like I'm on the right track but I think it's going to take at least a month and a lot of balls to get it feeling normal. No problem, I am nothing if not stubborn.

I'm now back home, having listened to Richard Russo's "Straight Man" while I was driving. He is really good at developing misfit male characters and much wiser female characters into stories. What a fine writer. And I bet he's never used a meaningless phrase like that last one as a sentence. I'll have to show him how to do that.

I'm in my chair, feet on the bed, typing away and slowly my eyes are drifting shut. It could very well be nap time, and I hope I don't get any entertainment nightmares.

Okay, I don't fall asleep. I watch YouTube videos, lots of them from Ellen Degeneres who has done amazing things for gay pride. I haven't done anything for gay pride. I'm one of those guys who says, "I've got a lot of gay friends," hoping to impress people with how nice I am. Hey, I was in show business. You can't be in show business without having gay friends. But I digress. Let's digress further and talk about pets.

MR. CLUELESS AND
HIS ANIMAL FRIENDS

At breakfast, Jintana and I talked about how her nieces are teenagers now and the fun part is over. Texting is far more important than we are and basically we're just drivers, people they say hello to on the way to and from school. When they were young, Kadjang and Awee would build a fort of pillows on the bed and then Kadjang would say, "You have to be the monster." Who could resist a role like that? I would growl and attack the fort and they would scream. I think it was my greatest role, academy award stuff.

Their dad, Chaipon, got a puppy at one point and this was problematic because the kids were really scared of dogs. This is logical because Thailand is filled with Soi (street) dogs and they are feral. They run wild and they can be dangerous. The puppy was named Thungnun, which translates as "MoneyPocket" and he was a handful. He was basically a soi dog and he grew up to be loud, scary, and a danger to the neighborhood. A few times I would walk out to the street to find terrified people standing there with Thungnun barking ferociously at them. He'd also chase motorbikes, most of them driven by kids, and try to bite the riders. Scary stuff.

We have a big yard and tried to keep him inside because we were afraid he would attack one of the village kids. Also, he would bark all night. We tried everything. I Googled, YouTubed, and tried every method of curing a vicious dog who barked all night.

One night we had a barbecue in the yard and he chased Kadjang (she was probably about eight at the time) around the yard. I tried to catch either her or the dog, but I couldn't and it was awful. She was really scared. We finally got the dog stopped.

Jintana's sister, Maew, lives with her husband, Ole, in Denmark and they love dogs, so when they came to visit they loved Thungnun and Ole built a dog house for him. Thungnun never set foot in it and became more and more unruly. One day he slipped out of his collar (he was a genius at that) and I tried to put it back on. He was twitchy and I tried to calm him down but then he bit my hand. It swelled up about double size and I had to go for rabies shots. When Maew and Ole came back for another visit, he bit Maew quite badly on the arm and was vicious, even with them. It was time to put him to sleep before he killed some little kid. They took him to the vet and got some pills. They didn't work. They took him back to the vet to put him to sleep and he still survived. He was a fighter, but two days after he got home, he lay down on the steps and died.

I felt sorry for him. I used to take him for walks, and when I was sure no one was around I'd let him run free in the field down the road from our house. But I never was able to work with him or get him used to a leash. We bought him dog toys and things to chew on. I tried to play fetch, but he never got the hang of that either. He'd get the tennis ball, but he wouldn't bring it back. Or if he did, he wouldn't let go of it, so fetch turned into "This is my ball and if you try to get it I'm going to bite your arm off." I never really liked that game.

So Thungnun died at about age 6 or 7. We felt sad at our lack of ability to sort him out, and I felt sorry for the neighbors, who had to spend years avoiding our street and years of endless nighttime barking. Now, Jintana's mom has a tiny little dog who seems quite happy and sane.

My history with pets wasn't that good. When we were little kids in Detroit, Michigan, my sister Nancy and I begged for a puppy. Finally we got one, a cocker spaniel puppy, and we promised to feed him and take care of him. This lasted about a week because we were little kids and soon the care of our dog fell mostly upon our mother. One day, a few months later, we came home from school and our cocker spaniel was gone. It was explained to us that he had to go because we didn't take care of it. Looking back, this seems borderline brutal to me, but I'm sure there's more to the story. I hope so.

There is more to the story. Nancy read this chapter and her memory is better. Here's her version:

> I have read part of your book and can tell you what I remember about the dog. We had made friends with a large, mellow, lovely stray mutt and probably pestered the parents to keep him. Instead, Mom decided we could have a dog, so she went and picked a registered blond cocker spaniel. We had no say in the matter. She even named it for us. "Ginger", if I remember right. The dog arrived, all hyper, and I remember climbing on the piano stool to get away from this barking maniac of a bitch. It may be my fault that they got rid of it. I'm sure I didn't take care of that dog. I did not like it. Mom did that a lot, I think. It was all about what she wanted.

A few years later we moved to Grosse Ile, Michigan and my folks bought a big old house with a garage that looked like a small barn. A couple of cats lived in the garage and in our yard and they were a part of life there but they had kittens and soon we had six or eight cats. One day, Mom took us for a walk and tried to explain we had to get rid of the cats. There was a lot of crying, and when we got back, the cats were gone. All of them.

Years later in Monterey I met my first wife, Leilani, and we got married. This is a long story and I'll just get to the pet part of that disaster. Leilani wanted a dog. We were on the road with me singing in bars, and a dog meant sneaking him into motels and all kinds of hassle. I explained this to her and two weeks later we had a dog. How does that happen?

It was a little one, and we traveled awhile with it. Then one day we noticed he was walking funny and shaking. We took it to the vet. He said it was distemper, and there was no cure. We had to have him put down. So then we bought a house in Ketchum, Idaho, and she wanted finches. I hate seeing birds in cages. To me, birds are meant to fly and be free. She insisted, so I built a huge bird cage out of two by fours and screen. At least the finches could fly a few feet. Leilani hated the cage because she couldn't get the finches to hop on her finger. I think the finches lasted longer than our marriage, which isn't saying much.

And finally, Satch. I got married again when I was forty, to Kelly. Actually, we weren't legally married but we were together 15 years, so I think it counts. She is a nice woman and she and her family had always had dogs. One day after we moved in together she persuaded me to take her to the pound and get a dog. The people there said the one we chose would be a small dog, maybe 30 pounds or so. Wrong. He grew to be really big. I got to name him, and I chose Satch, after Louis "Satchmo" Armstrong and Satch Saunders, the basketball player. Satch was neurotic and scary. Kelly had been with dogs all her life and she couldn't figure him out. I read books, tried to out-think him, and we failed to even get him to come when we called.

I'd be sitting peacefully, reading a book, and suddenly he would burst into frantic barking. At nothing. Maybe a dust mote or a sunbeam. I would levitate out of my chair and then wait for my heart to slow down.

We lived in a tiny house on high bank waterfront in Suquamish, Washington, across Puget Sound from Seattle. I used to take Satch down the long flight of steps to the beach and if there were no people I would let him run free. One day he disappeared behind a large rock and started barking furiously so I ran down there and he had an older couple treed on the rock, scared to death. I actually tackled the dog and got him back on the leash, apologizing profusely.

Kelly and I split after 15 years and Satch stayed with her. I saw him one time after that, old and half blind, and...quiet. Finally.

So you see, pets have not brought happiness to my life. They've brought sadness, bites, blood, rabies shots, fear for little kids around me, and when I was a kid, tears for when they were suddenly taken away. One more short note, Jintana is not enthused about dogs either. When she was a little girl (she's only five feet tall now so she must've been tiny) she got attacked by a soi dog and still has a scar over her eye. When we went to Bali on our honeymoon, we could not walk the streets because Bali has soi dogs too and they scared her.

All that being said, when Thungnun, the troubled Thai dog, died, we were all sad. And we wished we could've understood him.

This morning I saw a dog like him—brown, muscular, a soi dog—and it brought back memories. The good news was he didn't bite me.

NEW ORLEANS, DENNEYS, ESTONIA, THAI FOOD AND ME

We played golf this morning, my friend Joe and I and our two caddies. We teed off in the dark with the caddies again holding up cell phone lights. We had to get off first because the same two walking guys were waiting and if we let them go first they would hold us up.

Joe is a retired businessman now teaching math in a school here in Chiangmai. He's from New Orleans and wildly proud of LSU and Joe Borrows, the quarterback who led the school to the national championship this year. Joe the golfer has taught me a lot of New Orleans history and a lot about Creole food. I have forgotten most of it because listening has never been my strong point.

I have been to New Orleans a few times, once just after a freighter lost control on the river and took out a lot of the waterfront. The French Quarter is a great walking area, and ranks up there with my favorite walking cities—San Francisco, St. Petersburg, Istanbul, New York, Amsterdam and a few others. I worked cruise ships off and on for about 20 years at the end of my career and I learned early to avoid the tours and just get off and walk. Oh sure, I made mistakes. In Tallinn, Estonia, I got off the ship, turned left, and ended up in the most dismal place I'd ever seen. It was like Russia, with gray apartments, broken pavement, and surly people standing around. I thought why did the ship even bother stopping here? This is the worst port I've ever seen!

The next time we docked in Tallinn, I turned right and walked about twenty minutes to find a stunningly beautiful old town. I sat at an outdoor cafe, drank cappuccino and marveled at the old buildings and interesting people. I also saw all the passengers on tour. I bet they never found that dismal area I discovered.

So Joe and I played golf and I've converted him into a fast golfer. We played 18 holes in 2 1/2 hours, and it was quite pleasant. Then we met for breakfast at Danisa's, where we ate traditional Thai breakfast food—a cheeseburger for him and a Greek chicken wrap for me. Maybe he was a musician in a past life.

I do love Thai food, but maybe not the northern Thai food Jintana's family loves, which has spices that will blow off the top of your head. Her nieces' favorite game is to tell me something is not spicy and then laugh gaily when I turn red and gasp with tears streaming down my face.

Jintana's mom and I have an unspoken agreement, where she won't eat most western food and I won't eat a lot of blazing hot Thai food. She thinks ours is hopelessly bland and I think hers is lethal. Years ago I heard a great story about Japan when they'd had the Sarin gas attacks and one day the alarms went off, people evacuated, only to find a Thai family cooking dinner.

Jintana's mom does like waffles and spinach quiche and when Jintana and I go to breakfast I generally bring one or the other home for her.

Mike Neun

Later I had lunch and headed to the driving range, where I found swing thought number 589, which I'm sure will solve everything. The only problem is I can remember all the other 588 thoughts as I'm standing over the ball on the course and grow paralytic.

I had muesli, fruit and yogurt for lunch, and I should explain that if you spent 45 years on the road, you discover the great freedom of eating any food at any time. Want pesto pasta for breakfast? Go for it! Cereal for dinner? No problem. Pie ala mode any time of day? Highly recommended. Even better news is that Jintana is on board with this thinking. Lasagna for breakfast is just fine with her. In the early years of playing bars in the Northwest, I found pie and ice cream to be dependable in almost all restaurants at all times. I also found if you're playing towns like Spokane, Cheyenne, Helena, etc. and get off work at 2 a.m., you will soon have the Denny's menu memorized. Want to meet barroom musicians? Late night at Denny's was the place to go.

I know now I was lucky to have played those bars. There is no greater training than to have to fill up four hours a night with two hours worth of material. Comedians, especially beginners, have a terrible time getting stage time, scratching for five minutes here, ten minutes there, and it's no wonder it takes ten years to come up with 45 minutes of material. The Beatles filled 8 hours a night when they played that bar in Germany, and it was insane, but worth it. I played guitar and did folk music, but always tried to inject humorous songs and stories and those became my career later on.

I'm now back listening to the book, "Straight Man", in the car and thanking all the great authors who have made my life so much more enjoyable. Richard Russo, Walter Mosely, Robert B. Parker, John Steinbeck—there are too many to name but they enhanced my life during those long years on the road. I wonder if they ever sat down and said, "I'm going to write 60,000 words no matter what." I could've taught them how to set the bar really low.

Mike Neun

PARTY ANIMAL? MAYBE NOT.

Years ago my brother, Tim, and I were taking our morning walk to our favorite muffin place in Eugene, Oregon, when he blurted out, "I hate parties."

I was stunned. It never occurred to me that you could hate parties. Everyone loves parties. You get together with friends, drink and talk and dance and everyone has a good time, right? Humans love parties and if you don't, there's something wrong with you. It was at that point I realized there was something wrong with me. I went back over my modus operandi at parties, which was to drink too much, fake being a party animal, talk loudly, say all the wrong things (liquor gives you a wonderful freedom to do that), and when all else failed, find a book and go hide in the bathroom until people force you back out. Damn, I hated parties too! Tim was my party savior!

That being said, why would any sane introvert pick a job where you have to get up in front of lots of people and entertain them? I'll tell you why. Women. When it came to meeting women, being glib and saying slick things, sweeping them off their feet, I batted about .001. I could drive up to a singles bar in a Ferrari, walk in throwing hundred dollar bills, and come out alone. One day I realized that approaching women was not the way to go. The obvious answer was to get them to approach me. The Elvis solution. He had women trying to sleep with him all the time and I thought that was brilliant. I started with a ukulele, moved to banjo (possibly the world's worst chick magnet) and ended up with a 12-string guitar doing comedy songs and stories. Wrong again.

If you're a failed party animal, get an electric guitar and become a lead singer in a rock band. Bang. Women come to you. Yippee! Even bass players get lucky sometimes.

But, and this is a huge but, I'm not sure there is such a thing as comedy groupies. I'm sure the big stars—Dave Chappel, Chris Rock, Bill Burr—have no problem finding women, and I can also say that playing guitar and working bars was a giant step up for me. It bumped my average up to at least .200. In a world of studs, I was a utility infielder. And every time I'd meet a woman it would be in the last day or two of a gig and I'd have to leave town. So the wild entertainer life I dreamed of didn't quite pan out.

The book, *Quiet*, about introverts, was a giant revelation to me. I learned a huge part of humanity is not big on socializing. Sadly it was published 50 years too late. The worst for me was working cruise ships near the end of my career. Don't get me wrong, the jobs on ships probably saved my life. I was terminally lonely on the road, very close to joining a cult or setting up a meth lab, and suddenly that changed.

I was doing an opening act at Harrah's at Lake Tahoe and a guy came up back stage and asked, "Have you ever worked cruise ships?"

I said, "No."

"Do you want to?"

I said, "Sure, why not?"

It was a blessing for me.

This was in 1983 and my career was not on a fast track

to stardom. I was playing college concerts, PBS TV shows, conventions and casino show rooms as an opening act. The money was good, but the big time was not breaking down my door.

On ships I found other entertainers, people from exotic places like Greece, Russia, Turkey, Poland, Japan, etc., and when we traveled the world they would fill me in on all sorts of knowledge. It was a steep learning curve and the line I worked was arguably the best in the world, Royal Viking Line. Not only that, they had three ships—one in the Americas, one in Asia, and one in Europe. Once they discovered I was a good fit for their audiences, I could choose which cruises to work and I could see the world. Sensational. So, good money (and there were no expenses to speak of), people to hang out with, fascinating itineraries (ships don't go to North Dakota), and best of all, good show rooms with professional sound and lights. What could go wrong?

Cocktail parties. Formal dinners.

Part of the job was socializing with the passengers and I was a confirmed loner. I could fake it for awhile, but if I got invited to a cocktail party followed by a formal dinner, I was looking at 3 hours of socializing. Lots of times while wearing a tuxedo. Damn. I could do it. I could talk and not embarrass myself, I could choose the right fork, but for me it was the toughest part of the job. I love entertaining. Nothing beats a really good night on stage. I love seeing the world. I love making friends from distant places and learning stuff. I can walk through distant ports talking one-on-one with an interesting person and truly enjoy it. But deep in my heart, I'm uncomfortable with larger groups.

There was one other problem. The passengers on these ships ranged from upper class to corporate moguls to royalty. I know you'll be shocked to hear this, but it was not a liberal crowd. They once had a mock election on the ship and Republicans polled 90%. I, on the other hand, was an ex-hippie folksinger commie pinko godless humanist. I felt like a spy. In truth I wasn't quite as radical as a lot of my friends but I definitely leaned left and was not religious. The good news was that back then the U.S. wasn't as bitterly divided as it is now. I didn't throw my beliefs in their faces and they didn't throw theirs in mine. Well, not much.

At one meal, a member of the British nobility remarked that he thought Pinochet, the murderous Argentine dictator, was a great man. I guess my eyes widened in shock because his wife turned to me and winked. Ahah! Another undercover bleeding heart!

INDIAN FOOD WITH CANADIANS

I just watched a video of Tom House teaching football and baseball mechanics to pitchers and quarterbacks and again I'm enthused about the knowledge available to athletes these days. In the old days, a pitcher or quarterback could lose his career because of a tiny mechanical flaw, something that could've been easily fixed if anyone knew what the hell to do. I love golf, and every day when I go to the range or go play I know that if my back could take it I could practice enough to be a really good player. I also know there is absolutely no reason for an 80-year-old to try to become a good golfer, but I'm hooked and always have been.

The Tom House video inspired me to work more on golf. Maybe I'll work on footwork too, as my balance is not great at the finish. If you get to a good finish, the bottom of your swing should be at the right place, right? Unless you do that phony old-man finish where the swing stops at waist height and then you fake it on up to a Jason Day pose.

I'm going to the range now, maybe down to Haripunchai Golf Course. It's a long way but I have nothing to do and a good book to listen to in the car. I don't know how much longer I'll have the freedom of being able to drive, so I'm going to enjoy it while I can.

Okay, it's later in the day and the driving range at Haripunchai is the best in town. Beautiful grass, surrounded by trees, lots of yardage markers and you can see the ball really well against the green scenery. Well worth the 45-minute drive down the Super Highway even with it being under construction most of the way. They are widening it, putting in overpasses. If you keep going south on the Super Highway, in 8 hours you'll be in Bangkok. You can also go by train, which takes about 12 hours, but I've heard it's a pleasant trip, with sleeper cars for overnight travel.

Robin, a friend of ours from Canada, is leaving tomorrow and having Indian food tonight but we're not going. The restaurant is near the Sunday Walking Street and parking will be awful. Oops, change of plans. Jintana wants to go to the walking street and maybe her sister and the kids will want to go too so I guess we're going.

Jintana asks me what jacket to wear over her gray dress. She trusts my fashion sense. I have friends who would roll their eyes at this. Me? Fashion? Mr. jeans and tee shirts? On the other hand I worked luxury ships where people loved clothes and jewelry so hopefully some fashion sense rubbed off. I always go for the simple, the elegant. It's easy because Jintana looks good in anything.

Robin is an interesting guy. His brother is a golf pro in Kelowna and kind of a Yoda figure to the golfers in the area. The two of them run a driving range there and Robin comes here for the winters when the range is closed.

I seem to attract people like Robin, who is a big guy with an overpowering personality. I've never met his brother, but I heard that the pros he learned from as a kid once took him to the range, gave him thousands of balls, and told him to hit slow-motion 6-irons. I guess it worked. He became a great golfer, realized he didn't want to play tournaments, and is now regarded as a teaching legend by the Canadian pros here in Thailand.

Robin, on the other hand, went to Los Angeles, worked in a variety of jobs that involved leasing cars to stars, comedy club management, and a large intake of various drugs. He is now clean and sober, a believer in Buddhism, wildly extroverted, and a mainstay at Chiangmai's M-Sport driving range. He knows everyone there. He wears woven bracelets, long hair, hits balls barefoot, and loves to hug people. I'm not big on hugs, but when Robin sets his mind to it, there's not much you can do.

Last night at the Indian dinner he told me a Dave Chapelle story I'd never heard. According to Robin, when Chapelle's TV show was blowing up the airwaves, Oprah and Bill Cosby told him to quit because he was bringing down Black people. They said if he didn't quit, he'd never work again. I have no idea if this is true. It's ironic, though, because if anyone has brought down Black people, it was Cosby. I opened for him a couple of nights at Harrah's in Lake Tahoe. The headliner, a singer I can't remember, got sick and Cosby filled in because he and Bill Harrah were great friends. All I can remember is going to his dressing room afterwards and awkwardly telling him how much I admired his work. He didn't say much. Now I feel kind of stupid.

I also feel it's kind of silly to have idols because nobody can live up to that sort of adulation. Everyone has flaws and some are downright criminal. When we were in college we all knew Cosby routines and Newhart routines and Smothers Brothers songs. Michael Jordan said he developed his game by watching great basketball players and taking a little bit here and a little bit there. That's how we learned comedy and music. Then at some point you had to stop imitating and try to be different, be true to yourself.

This good news is that Chapelle is now back on top, Cosby is forever disgraced and evil, and my life is ending in a very good place with people I love.

Robin? He's leaving Chiangmai today and will be back next winter. At the dinner was his lady friend, Wan, his Canadian friend, Jeff the coffee roaster, and a young Thai couple, Ping and his girlfriend whose name I can't remember. I've played golf with Jeff twice and enjoyed it. Last night, sadly, I also found he likes Trump and hates Trudeau, so we're not quite in tune politically. My Saturday partner, Joe, also revealed he is a Trumpster, so I feel like I'm back on cruise ships. Luckily, most of the people at the bridge club are commie pinko leftists. I have achieved balance in my life.

Ping, the Thai guy, is a pro Robin met at the M-Sport range. He's young, very handsome, hits the ball over 300 yards, and has a beautiful girl friend. Other than that, his life probably sucks. Jintana and I think they both come from a lot of money and they seemed quite nice. Wan, the lady with Robin, assured Jintana that she and Robin were just friends. We thought this was probably right as he would be a bit overwhelming to a Thai person.

I say all this having no clue what other people think of me. Who does? I know raving assholes who think everyone likes them. It's a humbling thought. At dinner, Robin told Ping I had a beautiful golf swing and that I'd been a comedian and he could find my stuff on YouTube. I said something self-deprecating and Robin said I should just say thank you. He's probably right.

Afterwards, Jintana and I walked over to the Walking Street. We passed Alice's Place, which has an open mic on Sundays and I'd thought of checking it out. I looked, and

36 Mike Neun

realized it would be a tough room to work. Chairs facing away from the stage, bad sight lines, the usual bar setup. I worked lots of those places over the early years and they were always a struggle, so I can chalk this off the list.

I've played three or four open mics here in Chiangmai, with varying degrees of success. I found I'm pretty useless with Thai people, even if they speak English, because my stuff is based on word play. I've also never been good in loud bars because I love understated comedy and loud rooms are best handled by overpowering entertainers. When I worked bars, I figured I could get the crowd calmed down about two or three nights out of six, and those nights would be fun. The others were just earning a living.

Oddly, there is a country song I wrote that works well here. In my years on stage that song was just a middle-of-the-act piece of material but here it is big time. I'm guessing the people who retire here are ex-army, ex-police, ex-blue-collar workers, and country music is a common ground. Also, the song is pretty jokey, with lots of punch lines, so that works too.

Now, however, I don't do open mics because they start too late and I go to bed early. It's a lot of work to stay up late, drive into town, lug a guitar into a bar, and do a song or two. I think my stage career is over.

It is the morning after the Indian dinner. On YouTube I watch a video about the writing and recording of "Bridge over Troubled Waters" and then two songs from Simon and Garfunkel's concert in Central Park. They are so pure in tone and the words and melodies are astounding. I was so lucky to be alive in their heyday.

Jintana changes the quilt. I never think of changing the quilt. She takes one side, I take the other. We're a team. Outside, birds are chirping.

The birds in Thailand make different noises. Exotic. I first noticed when I played Green Valley Golf Course. When I first came to Chiangmai it was a great golf course. Interesting, well kept. Now it is worn out from thousands of rounds and I haven't played it in years. The caddies still have the same blue uniforms, kind of tacky really. A smart owner would change those uniforms. My caddy at Green Valley, Aire, was a fine lady too. She endured my attempts to play in leagues during the early years, again in the afternoons. She kept her head when I was losing mine over bad shots and combative playing partners. She was one of the great people I've met here but she went with her boyfriend to work at a crocodile farm tourist attraction. I missed her a lot.

Jintana sits across from me. Her hair is curly, permed, and at first I didn't like it. Now I'm used to it and it looks good. She is naturally beautiful, and I love to watch her when she sleeps. No makeup, just a perfect face, peaceful.

I look at my bare feet propped up on the bed. Not smart. Old man feet, with a big bunion on my right foot, probably from too small shoes when I was a kid. I am thankful for shoes. My feet can hide.

In ten minutes I will drive Kadjang to school. Then I will meet Jintana for breakfast. The Super Bowl is on right now, but we have no TV set, no cable. We watch everything on our iPads, mostly Netflix and YouTube. No commercials. I will watch the Super Bowl highlights later.

In the U.S. the Super Bowl is like Christmas. The lead-up is so overpowering, the reality has to be a letdown. In this one, I want both teams to win. Both coaches are excellent and the players are too. But there is no way I would sit through 4 hours of commercials, halftime extravaganza, patriotic opening ceremonies, etc. to watch about 15 minutes of real action. That's right, in an average 60-minute game there's about 15 minutes of action.

Mike Neun

I am back home now, after a breakfast set of eggs, sausage, potatoes and English muffin. Jintana and I always split a breakfast order, as half seems about right for us.

Novak Djokovic won the Australian Open. Good. He has a great sense of humor so I root for him. Federer and Nadal do too, so we are living in a golden age of tennis stars who can laugh. The young women tennis stars seem really cheerful and well-spoken also. Naomi Osaka after the U.S. Open final with Serena Williams was the ultimate class act.

BIGFOOT HITS THE GOLF MALL

This morning the alarm woke me at 5:20 and I got up, put water in the hot water kettle, and cut myself a half of a danish I got yesterday at Nana Bakery. When I first came to Chiangmai, baked goods were pretty sketchy. Apparently asian people like bread that is soft, sweet, and has a soft crust. I, on the other hand, am hooked on French and Italian bread, anything with a thick crust.

Two big things have changed in Chiangmai over the years. There are coffee shops everywhere and we have some good bakeries. Nana is located about four miles from our house at a shopping center called Kad Falang. That translates as "foreigners' market." Nana has croissants, danish, baguettes, dark rolls and everything else I could desire. Yippee.

So I woke up, put on the hot water and ate the danish. I can't drink coffee before golf because I have prostate cancer. Diagnosed 15 years ago and I went through the operation and then radiation when they found the operation didn't get it all. Exciting, right? Getting to hear an old fart talk about medical problems? Wait, there's more!

For 15 years I've taken hormone shots to reduce testosterone, which carries the cancer. Every three months

I get an expensive shot and as a bonus prize I get to lose body hair (I don't hang out in locker rooms), have hot flashes (Never, ever think a woman is exaggerating when she complains about them. Hot flashes suck), and, wait for it, mood swings.

I had mood swings before the shots. Ask any woman I've ever been with. Ask anyone I've played golf with. Ask anyone who's seen me after a bad show. I can go dark, and it's not pretty.

Digress much? Hell yes, I was talking about my morning wasn't I. So I put on two shirts and a sweat shirt, and head out into 15 degree darkness for a solitary round of golf. By the second hole the sun will be rising. I'm enthused, because yesterday at the range I found if I make a fuller turn on my backswing I can find an extra ten yards. I can't wait.

North Hills is a short drive and I pull up to the front entrance to drop off my bag. I park the car and put on my new golf shoes. There are no size twelves in all of Chiangmai, so I had to go on a family trip to Bangkok to find some. Jintana, a Buddhist, works at a Christian University and that's kind of weird but Thai people are much less strident about these things. The university has connections with a Christian hotel in Bangkok so we stay there when we go down. There are Bibles in the drawers and lots of Christian stuff. I feel a bit strange but the people are nice and it's a perfect location in the heart of town. It's also perfect because it's amazingly cheap and about a 5-minute walk to the golf mall.

Taniya Plaza is a mall in Bangkok with five floors of nothing but golf stores. Guess how many size twelve golf shoes were in that mall? Two. With Jintana's prodding I bought the expensive Mizunos because neither of us could stand the blue camouflage design on the cheaper Adidas. Oh well, probably my last pair and they would keep my feet dry in my early-morning rounds when the grass is wet.

Mike Neun

Now, back at North Hill with my new shoes on, I lock the car and go pay green fees. Then I head out to the kiosk that houses the starter and snack stand. Ploy, my caddy, is waiting and today there are no other early golfers. I can wait for almost dawn before I tee off. I use my new swing, hit it pretty well, and do the same on my second shot. Then I chunk one. Damn. I go on to play badly, lots of sideways shots, and by the time it's over I realize my extra distance has cost me three balls in the water. I love golf.

When I finished, a golfer just going out looked at his watch. He couldn't believe I was finished. It was 8:30 a.m.

Afterwards I was supposed to meet my friend John.

John is my age and a better player but I finally put a stop to our games together. He likes to play slowly, asking the caddy where every trap and tree is, the exact distance, then a practice swing or two, then a very careful setting up and a slow swing with lots of wrist break and (this pisses me off no end) great contact.

He has one swing thought which he's repeated about 3000 times in our friendship (I never exaggerate), that if you swing slowly the ball will go farther. Being a blatant contrarian, this only spurs me on to swing faster and harder. My argument is, show me a PGA tour player who swings slowly. I'm 80 years old, and if I swing any slower I'll be at full stop. I haven't compressed a ball in 20 years. So my theory is to swing hard in case I hit it.

I finally stopped our games because of the speed tug of war. He compromised by going faster, I compromised by going slower, but it was uncomfortable. We still meet for the occasional meal and this morning I finished, went home and showered and then drove to Chez Nous for breakfast. You guessed it, a French bakery with great food. Being a musician I had pesto pasta for breakfast. I told John I was trying to make a better turn on my backswing, and he told me I might want to try swinging slower. 3001.

John is a retired banker, very successful, who started in Canada, lived a few years in Jamaica, and ended up in Australia. He comes to Thailand and Kuala Lompur in the winter months. I've seen pictures of him when he was young, and I'm thinking he was a stud. He also is a mild Trump supporter, so we walk on eggs when we talk politics. We agree on some things, but not on others.

This morning he told me a story about his brief encounter with Hapsburg royalty. I think the first rule of conversation is to use his story time to come up with a story of my own, but I think this is close to what he said: Apparently the Hapsburg heirs came to Australia and he was asked to escort the lady to a dinner. She learned he was planning a trip to Europe and invited him to come visit. He took that with a grain of salt, but surprise, the invitation held up. He and his Australian buddy, a cockney guy, met them at their villa and they were invited to dinner the next night at a tiny restaurant by the sea, renowned for their fresh fish. Apparently John's friend frowned and they didn't think he liked fish. They switched all their plans and reservations and went instead to an elegant dinner at a hunting lodge in this hills, with lots of waiters and a large table of guests. The waiter asked John's friend what he'd like to order, and the guy said, "I'll have the fish.."

He never lived it down.

John the banker thinks the worst thing that happened to the corporate economy was stock options. We agree on that and quite a few economic issues but we're still far apart politically. He'd watched the Super Bowl with friends and I couldn't wait to mention Trump's tweet of congratulations to the Chiefs and the great state of Kansas. We have a president who doesn't know the team represents Kansa City, Missouri.

It's now about 4:30 p.m. and I'm at Danisa's restaurant trying to write, but I'm thrown off my game by a foreign (I

Mike Neun

have no idea of nationality) woman who just won the Short Shorts of the Year award. I try not to stare, and fail.

I am debating whether to have something to eat. I'm debating whether to give up golf and end the misery. I'm debating my complete inability to change the world. Once again I realize I'm a tiny, tiny speck in the universe. I have all the power of a dust mote in a hurricane.

WHY YES, I CAN SHOOT A JUMP SHOT

For me, the best sports show on TV was Open Court. It had everything. Stories, lots of humor, great inside knowledge, and the beauty is you can still find it on YouTube.

I played basketball in high school and I had no clue how hard you had to practice to be really good. I thought I was practicing a lot but I was doing about 50% of what it would've taken to just be a good high school player. I was at a tiny high school. Grosse Ile High School, on an island in the Detroit River, had about 200 students and was a wonderful school. We had five good basketball players and I wasn't one of them. A smart kid would've learned to dribble with his left hand and shoot jump shots moving in either direction. All I could do decently was rebound. I made the team, but I never played meaningful minutes. Garbage time was my life.

I still watch basketball and I'm a Golden State Warriors fan because I love their style of play. Even now, with their stars injured and a weak lineup, they still move the ball and put out effort. LaBron James is the best player in the league, but I don't care if I ever see a team clear out one side so their star can go one-on-one and score. Boring. My early heroes were Magic Johnson and Larry Bird because they made the players around them better.

You know which old-time comedian did that? Jack Benny. I didn't realize it until I read it somewhere, but on his radio and TV shows, Benny never took the punch lines! You can go back and watch or listen. Everyone's making fun of him, and he's reacting. He was the ultimate comedy team player. How cool is that?

So I know two things about excellence. One, none of us mortal people know how much work you have to put in to be the best in the world. And two, there are people who are the best in the world, but are also selfish and mean-spirited. I don't admire them. I admire talent, skill, and decency. By the way, I don't think LaBron James is mean-spirited or selfish and I guess the Lakers are now playing more team ball but I still like the Warriors.

I wish I knew who the decent golfers are. I'd hate to be rooting for a jerk, but I've probably done it because I just don't have the information. I'm sure there are top golfers out there who are great, thoughtful people, and there are others who are racist, misogynistic bastards, and I know that it will be covered up. Oh well. I solve it by always rooting for underdogs, and never, ever betting on sports. If you love underdogs and bet on sports, you will end up a street person.

Mike Neun

BRIDGE, THE BEST WAY TO LOWER YOUR GRADE POINT

I went back to the bridge club today. I know what you're thinking. Oh boy! The card game old people played before video games. We're talking fun!

I'll be brief.

I quit bridge about a month ago because I overdosed. As usual, if I get into a game I want to win. Then I realize some other people will always be better because of little things, like the ability to count to 13.

Here's a secret.

All human games, all music, all comedy, all art forms, are just plain silly. Wow, you put a ball in a hoop and make 30 million a year! Tell me that's not silly. You sat in a room and played guitar 8 hours a day until your fingers bled and you had to super glue the callouses back on. Tell me that's a form of sanity. Yeah, right. I have a friend, Mark Nizer, who is the best, most inventive juggler I've ever seen. His theory was that all mastery arises from inner pain. You have to have some form of inner pain to stand in a garage eight hours a day juggling stuff.

Bridge. A card game. Actually it's a fascinating card game my parents played and I thought was stupid until I learned it in college and lowered my grade point a couple notches. I'd play at lunch, and then not go to my next class because I was sitting on a slam hand and couldn't walk away.

After college I sang in bars until I got drafted. Being smart, when they asked about skills, I said I could type 60 words a minute. My thinking was that I'd never seen a typewriter near the front lines. 60 words a minute? Not even close, but it got me stationed as a clerk at Fort Ord. Not only that, I got put in an office with two other guys who could type. As a result, we could do our work in a couple of hours. We typed allotments, and we could run through a company in about an hour. Another hour to set them up and we were done.

So, what to do with the other 6 hours?

Those two guys, and the lieutenant who ran the office played, you guessed it, bridge. We were the only office in the army that had a bridge club.

Good people too. Lieutenant Phil Greenspun was the only officer I knew who got pissed off if you saluted him, because he had to salute back. If you saluted him when no one was looking he would give you the finger.

Andy Sarkany (I'm not sure of his last name, I haven't thought of him in years) was the quiet guy. I think he had a degree in history, and wouldn't be surprised if he became very successful.

Doug Wickline was a little guy, fiercely competitive, and not just a bridge player but a golfer too. And not just any golfer. He had the best hustler swing I ever saw. His right elbow flew out at the top of his backswing, he came over the top, his shots started low and looked like a hacker's slice, and he putted with a 2-dollar putter he found at the Salvation Army. You knew, you just knew, he was easy money. Wrong.

50   Mike Neun

He was a hell of a golfer. And a good bridge player.

All of us were draftees. All of us got in before Vietnam heated up. And every day we played bridge.

I didn't play bridge much after the army, but twenty years later I started working cruise ships and they had bridge games. I learned two things. One, passengers were surprised by a comedian who could play decent bridge. Two, we had bridge lecturers come on board and a lot of them were world-class players. I loved it.

Best of all, bridge had become a better game over the years. In the old days, if you had bad cards, you got bored to death while the other team won hand after hand. Ah, but experts found that bad hands weren't that bad after all. Long suits were valuable, both to play and to bid to get in the way of opponents bidding. Duplicate and IMP scoring meant you could compare results with people playing the same hands. In short, it's become the best card game I've ever played.

Now, I play at the Bridge Club of Chiangmai and it's been a lifesaver. There's not much to do on a blazing hot Thai afternoon and the air-conditioned bridge club solved that. I've been playing about ten years and I've made lots of friends there. I still love bridge. I'm not the best player but I'm not bad and even though I overdose now and then I always find I enjoy it when I get back. I'm just going to play less often.

THE FALL OF THE ROMAN EMPIRE AND ME

A friend of mine posted a list on Facebook of things that contributed to the fall of Rome and I disagreed with about half of them so I did some research. My idea of research is to go on YouTube, find university lectures about Rome, and listen to them when I drive to the golf course or pick up kids.

So now I'm the poster boy for A Little Knowledge is a Dangerous Thing. I found that historians have come up with over 200 reasons for the fall of Rome, and that people of any political persuasion can cherry pick them to justify their beliefs. All I'm going to do is point out a couple of things I didn't know. One is that in the final days of the empire there was a bad winter and the Rhine River froze over. The Romans had the crossings and bridges fortified, but that year the barbarians could just walk across the ice between the fortifications. Bad news for the Romans.

I also didn't know that the barbarians had assimilated into the Roman armies and that some of the armies were commanded by barbarians.

I didn't know that the barbarians were caught between the Huns in the east and the Romans in the west. Attila the Hun was an overpowering motive to march west.

My deep studies, well over three hours, also reinforced my theory that people who love strong man rulers are doomed to disappointment. If you like dictators, emperors, tzars or kings, your chances of getting a good one are tiny.

Rome had that problem. Lots of emperors, most of them useless or horrible, and the empire crumbled.

My personal feeling is that Rome had bad leadership, was overextended and fell apart economically, and like all human enterprises, had a life cycle that went through youth, middle age and old age. Empires rise and fall. They get old and corrupt.

Can we equate that to modern times? I'm sure we can learn lessons, but I'm not sure anyone in power will use them. America is an empire, and there's nothing to say it won't go through the same process. There is definitely a huge element of corruption, with money having far too much influence in elections and government. There is also an element of over-extension, where our vast military forces are becoming harder to support economically. It's definitely possible that some other empire will rise to power. Historically it always happens.

Ah, but that's too depressing. Let's talk waffles.

Jintana and I split a waffle and fruit for breakfast. Perfect. We also had a problem with money, about borrowing some to fix up the house. I have this awesome feeling I handled it more wisely than usual, where I wrote down my misgivings and said we should wait to talk about them for awhile so we can be calm and rational. That would never have occurred to me in the past. I would've jumped in and tried to settle it immediately, thereby setting up a confrontation. We'll see if I actually accomplished anything.

Mike Neun

Also this morning I listened to Jordan Peterson (along with Joe Rogan and another guy whose name I don't know but was very erudite) and Peterson talked about a curve that held true in all forms of human endeavor. In every form of production, there are a tiny few who are more creative and work harder than everyone else. They achieve huge success and huge rewards, basically the 1%. Then there are those who do almost as well, so that they achieve great rewards also. And on down the line to those at the bottom who create absolutely nothing and starve to death.

My question is, do the rewards have to be absolutely in line with creativity and productivity? In other words, wouldn't truly smart people realize that if you're at the top you don't have to take all the spoils? Couldn't you live a good life on, say, a million dollars a year and spread the rest around to your employees, or those who are starving? I'm not saying we have to take money from the rich, I'm saying in an advanced, truly intelligent society, people at the top might disconnect absolute achievement from absolute reward. For their own benefit, they might put a personal cap on rewards and share the rest. Then they would be less vulnerable to the masses with torches and pitchforks.

Minimalism comes into play here. Even if you're wildly talented and successful, what do you actually need to live a good life? A truly smart person would figure that out and then decide what to do with the rest of the money. So maybe the solution is to educate the rich. Teach them what a truly successful lifestyle is. And isn't. It's all about what you do, not what you have.

Everyone can learn this.

You don't have to have a big house, a hot car, a home studio, a pool, or whatever. You can live a better life simply than you can by spending millions on yourself.

Life on the road taught me this.

I can live in a hotel room. That's all I need. A bed, a bathroom, and that's it. If I want to cook, I'm good with a hot plate or a microwave. I don't like to cook, and in Thailand I'm in hog heaven. The street food here is nourishing, cheap, and plentiful. Anyway, life on the road taught me my own minimalism.

For some reason, most rich people go down that same luxury path and I submit that it's not a good life. Really. Someone has to teach them that, and someone has to teach the middle class not to go broke trying to imitate the rich. Seriously. You can have way more fun sailing a dingy than you can drinking on a yacht. You can have as much fun playing a public golf course as you can playing Pebble Beach. I know, I've done both. If you go on a luxury cruise, you know who has the best parties? The crew.

Minimalism. Forget having stuff. Doing stuff is a hundred times more fun. It will bring you much more joy and fulfillment. Then, being human, you can also find the joy of sharing your largess with people who need it way more than you, and that will make you happier than owning a private jet.

So I think the rich should pay their fair share of taxes, but it's more important to teach them the emptiness of their lifestyles. I know, I spent most of twenty years entertaining on luxury cruise ships. I studied the lifestyle, and I sincerely liked mine better. I was doing a job I loved and hanging out with fellow entertainers. The downside? I had to dress up a lot. Rich people love to dress up and I will never understand that concept either. I can have way more fun in jeans and tee shirt than I can in a tuxedo. Basically, I would've had just as much fun singing in coffeehouses but it's hard to live on ten bucks a night. I worked the ships because it was a job, it paid well I could save money, and I wasn't as lonely as I was on the road in the U.S. Also I got to see the world and hang

Mike Neun

out with really interesting people. I've never been rich, and I don't miss it at all. I wouldn't trade my life for anything.

Oh wait, at the little bar down the road they're playing loud karaoke music. I might trade part of my life for a mute button.

Noise is a big part of Thai life. Sound trucks are normal, driving around advertising something very loudly. A Thai mall usually features a very loud show in the main floor, or loud music. When I took the family back to the states, we went into an American mall and it felt like a morgue. In Thailand also, poor people go to malls just for the air conditioning, so they're generally crowded, noisy and alive.

In villages, the head man generally makes announcements over a loudspeaker system at random times. It's part of life. And now we come to weddings, funerals and holidays. All are excuses for blasting out loud music and karaoke and setting off fireworks. I'm not talking ladyfingers here, I'm talking big Chinese skyrockets, bombs, whatever makes the most noise. One of my first memories of Thailand was being in a Bangkok bar on New Years when people were setting off skyrockets INSIDE the bar. That's right, rockets were bouncing off the walls and zipping between your legs. Duck and cover! Thai people love fireworks, so holidays sound like WWII. I also think that because they do it all the time, pets get used to it and it's not traumatic, but I may be wrong. I know the soi dogs just go about their business.

Normal Thai parties are noisy too, and usually feature Karaoke. Let me tell you about Thai parties, because I don't like parties and yet I have to admit Thai people do them the best. You go to a Thai party and nobody cares what you do. You can sing, dance, get drunk, talk, not talk, play with dogs, run around, or go sit in a corner and read a book. I think it's just wonderful. And the dress code is generally whatever you've got on at the time. Shorts, flip flops, tee shirts, dresses, make up, no makeup, whatever the hell you want. And there will be food. There will be enough food to feed an army. Tables bending under the weight of food. And you can eat whenever you please, whatever you please. There is a wonderful freedom to it all and I highly recommend Thai parties. But they will be noisy. And there might be fireworks.

The downside is that Chinese fireworks are not dependable. When Jintana and I got married, we had a combination wedding and housewarming at the new house her family had built. I like Thai weddings, as they are less elaborate than the ones back home. I'm not going to go into the ceremony now, but it was cheerful and involved monks chanting and people filing by tying strings to our wrists while giving us their blessings. Afterwards they took us upstairs to lie on a bed filled with rose petals. We hugged and everyone laughed and took pictures.

At the party that followed, everyone had a good time until one of the Chinese firework bombs didn't go off. One of Jintana's cousins, very drunk, staggered over to see what was wrong and it blew up. He died a couple of days later and as a result, the new house had a ghost problem. None of the family could move into it for about two years and Jintana and I lived in my cheap apartment (I'm a minimalist, remember?) in town. Later, we and the rest of the family moved into the house, and we've lived there ever since.

I've never seen the cousin's ghost.

Mike Neun

HOW TO WRITE A JOKE

Hah! If I'd figured that out I'd still be working, basking in new material and dazzling audiences. No, you have to find someone smarter than me to get that answer.

I've written stuff all my life and I'm happy writing this, no matter how it turns out. But I have to admit I like golf more. When I go to a driving range or a golf course I always have something new I want to try out. I can't wait to see if it works. And if it fails miserably, no problem, because I'll have some new cure to work on the next day.

With writing, I never had that. I wrote comedy for a living because that's what I did on stage and all comedians are desperate for material. I used the monkey-on-the-typewriter technique. I figured if I wrote every day, for three or four hours, I'd come up with something funny, even if it was just by chance. I also figured I could write about something serious and keep writing about it until the seriousness would break down and I'd have to laugh. Both techniques were wildly undependable.

I think great comedians have some idea of joke structure and some method of coming up with new material that they can count on. I didn't have that. I just wrote. At first I liked felt-tipped pens and notebooks, and I would write freestyle, going wherever my mind would take me. Later on I switched to laptop computers so I could write lots more pages. Every now and then a nugget would appear and I'd get mad because I had no idea how to do it again. In the end I wrote four hours a day. That was my discipline. I finally retired when I realized I wasn't coming up with anything new.

Ever since I retired I've kept writing, going in all directions. I've tried writing comedy material, short stories, books, blogs, whatever and I haven't come up with anything I really liked. Wait, I take that back. Some of my Facebook posts are inventive. So this book is my latest challenge. I will finish!

By the way, I listened to more of that Joe Rogan/ Jordan Peterson/guy-who's-name-I-still-haven't-figured-out discussion and Peterson said a couple of interesting things. One, he said a universal basic income was a terrible idea because what people needed more than money was a feeling of purpose. A usefulness. A job. I can see that.

But then he said that Canadians had more entre-preneurial startups than the U.S. and one reason was that Canadians had health care. They didn't have to stick to crappy jobs just to keep their health insurance. And my thought was health care is like universal basic income. Both offer you security if you want to start something new.

Even Peterson, a believer in capitalism, admits that the U.S. healthcare system sucks. And costs more. It works brilliantly for rich people, but for middle-class people and lower-class people, it sucks.

Anyway, it is Rogan's show number 1006 and it's really thought provoking.

THE GREAT COMEDIAN FIGHT
IN BUTTE, MONTANA

B rian and I, under the name Mike and Brian, an Act as Exciting as its Name, were playing the Golden Bell bar in Billings, Montana. As I remember, the stage was on the back bar, so between us and the crowd was the bar, the bartenders, etc. Our act was kind of a poor man's Smothers Brothers, with Brian as the comedian and me as a straight man who didn't want to be a straight man. Brian could do dialects, physical comedy and improv—all the things I couldn't do. I could write and perform stuff. Songs, bits, and so on.

Anyway, after a good night some of our friends invited us to a party in Butte. For those of you not familiar with Montana, Butte was a mining town, to the point where they actually moved downtown so they could dig for copper. It was known as tough, because miners are tough.

A digression here.

Oscar Wilde, the immensely talented, flamboyantly gay, author/playwright, once toured the mining camps in Montana, Wyoming, and other wild west states giving lectures. People worried he'd have a terrible time with the rough, fight-loving miners but not only did his lectures go well, he won the miners over by drinking them under the table.

Digression two.

I spent three or four years working in ice shows. The first was with Peggy Fleming, called A Concert on Ice, and I would walk out onto the ice (usually in a theater in-the-round) and do 15 minutes of comedy. We toured the east coast, then went to Sun Valley, Idaho, to do a couple shows before we did Christmas at Harrah's Casino in Lake Tahoe.

At the time I lived in Ketchum, Idaho, which is two miles down the road from Sun Valley and was home to cowboys, skiers, and tourists. The bars were basically cowboy bars and people like me wearing jeans and Pendleton shirts pretending to be cowboys. Lots of drinking, swearing, smoking, pool shooting and so on.

We did the show in Sun Valley at the outdoor rink, and the boy skaters announced they were going bar hopping in Ketchum. Except for one ex-hockey player who found he could make more money figure skating, the boy skaters were quite gay and really fun to be with. Astounding senses of humor, very bitchy. So they were going to go hit the cowboy bars and I thought that was a really bad idea. There was no way I was going to change their minds, so I watched them head out.

Well, I was dead wrong. They had a wonderful time drinking with the cowboys and there was no trouble at all. Later I saw the movie, Priscilla, Queen of the Desert, and it reminded me of those tours. It's a classic and if you haven't seen it you owe it to yourself to find it. Trust me.

End of Digression, back to the big fight.

Brian and I plus four others piled into a car and headed to the party in Butte. It was in a house, and at the time I handled parties by getting drunk and passing out. What

Mike Neun

better way to avoid social interaction? So I sat in an easy chair with a bottle of Jim Beam and pounded it down while people partied.

Then a guy I'd never seen before came up and said, "You're going out with my girl."

I'd gone out a couple of times with a really great woman in Billings named Julie but there'd been no mention of a boyfriend and she wasn't with me that night. I guessed that was who he was talking about, so I looked up and said, "Okay. I'm going out with your girl."

I'm an agreeable drunk.

He said, "We're going to fight."

I never fight. Fighting is stupid. And when do you do stupid things? When you've downed half a bottle of Jim Beam. Suddenly I was John Wayne and said, "Okay, let's fight."

I got up and staggered outside, because in all the movies that's how it's done. The two fighters walk outside, the crowd gathers and the hero (me) beats the crap out of the bad guy. Well, he hadn't read the script. I walked outside and it was a blizzard, snow coming down sideways, and really cold. The bad guy didn't come out! No one did.

After awhile I thought screw this, and went over to the car, climbed in the back seat and passed out.

What I didn't know was that Brian had leaped into improv action when he saw this fight thing setting up. When I walked out, he announced, "That's no fun! We should all fight!"

Then he went around the room pairing up people. "You fight him! You two fight! You two girls fight! Everybody fights!" Apparently it was quite funny.

Then he went up to the biggest guy in the room and said, "You and I are going to fight." It was a great comic moment, because Brian was small, and had lost his hair at a young age. So this little bald guy was going to fight the biggest guy in Butte, Montana. It should've been a crowd-pleasing, fun moment, but the big guy had no sense of humor and clocked Brian.

He put his hand up to protect his face, and the punch broke his thumb and cut his lip quite badly. Brian didn't know his thumb was broken, he just knew it hurt and that his lip was all bloody.

Well that was the end of the big fight, cooler heads prevailed, and our group piled into the car, surprised to find me passed out in the back seat, and drove back to Billings.

On the way, one of our group turned out to be from the reservation and a warrior. He loudly proclaimed that we had to go pick up some of his friends and go back and clean house in Butte. We talked him down.

We flew back to Portland the next day, and it must've been a small plane because I have a mental picture of Brian's wife waiting at the foot of the steps, seeing Brian with a bandaged hand and lip, putting her hands on her hips and saying, "Oh Brian."

Mike Neun

WHY YES, I AM A VEGAS ACT.

You know those books where big stars tell show business stories about all the other big stars and life at the top? Well this isn't one of them. I was never a big star.

Let's start with Las Vegas.

I was young, I'd done opening acts in Reno and Lake Tahoe at Harrah's casinos which were truly first class with ideal show rooms, but I'd never played Las Vegas. Reno and Tahoe felt good to me because Reno was kind of a cowboy town and Tahoe was a ski resort. I was at home in both situations because of my Ketchum-Sun Valley days. Cowboys and skiers. My people.

Las Vegas? No way. I made fun of Las Vegas shows. The feathers, the smoke, the glitter, the big spenders, Wayne Newton—I was the opposite of all that.

One day my manager called and said, "Great news! You're going to open for Ann Margret at Caesar's Palace in Las Vegas!"

I said what any folksinger/comedian would say. "No chance in hell! I'm not going."

I went on to explain I was not a Las Vegas act, I didn't belong, I would bomb, and I didn't want to do it. A month later I was on a plane to Las Vegas to open for Ann Margret.

We need some background here.

About a year earlier, I'd bombed on the Tonight Show with Johnny Carson. Oh sure, Brian was there too but it was me who forgot the words to a song that I had written. Let me repeat that. I forgot the words to a song I HAD WRITTEN. In front of millions! It was the worst night of my life, if you discount a couple of divorces, so I wasn't full of confidence. I just wanted to do my shows in comfortable surroundings, make money, have a good time, and become better at comedy.

Nope, wasn't going to happen. I was on a plane to Las Vegas, to the biggest casino at that time, Caesar's Palace, to open for the most Las Vegas show ever produced. Huge dance numbers, big stage effects, wild costumes and Ann Margret, a super star. And before all that, I was going to walk out alone on that stage, with my guitar, sit on a stool, and do understated humor. Sure! That'll work!

I got off the plane, went to the baggage area to pick up my guitar and suitcase, and they weren't there. The airlines had lost my luggage. No guitar, no clothes, and I was going on stage that night.

So I walked out and there was a stretch limo to pick me up. It was all too much. I got to Caesar's Palace, went to the show room where they were setting up, and explained what happened. Roger Smith, Ann Margret's husband, said, "No problem. We'll find a guitar."

I said, "Well, there is one problem, I play a 12-string."

He said, "We'll find something. Now go to the men's store here at Caesar's and find some clothes to wear tonight. Charge them to the show.

I went to the store, and it was like going to Rodeo Drive. Every item had a designer name, and the prices were through the roof. He told me to just charge it to the show, so I got clothes. Gucci loafers, the only ones that fit, $700. That was in the 1970s. I'd never owned a pair of shoes that cost more than 35 bucks. Pants? Nothing but the best, but they were like golf slacks, with pleats, and I would never, ever buy a pair like that. Next, a shirt, a sweater, and the bill took my breath away.

I went back to the showroom and they'd dug up a 12-string guitar that belonged to one of the stagehands. Let me tell you about 12-string guitars. The strings exert a huge amount of force when they are tightened up, and when you have 12 of them, and tune them up to pitch, a cheap guitar will fold in half. As a result, most 12-strings are tuned down a third, which means the strings aren't as tight, and you don't snap off the neck. But, and this is a huge but, every song is now in a different key! My guitar was a Martin D-41, top of the line, and you could tune it up to pitch. This one? I didn't think so. I talked to the stagehand and he was cool. He said go for it, I think the guitar can take it. So we gave it a shot and the guitar didn't snap in half. I assumed it would wait till the middle of my set to do that.

So that night, terrified, I walked out on stage to open the Ann Margret show in golf slacks, Gucci loafers, a cashmere sweater, carrying a strange guitar that could blow up at any time, and did my 17 minutes. I have no memory of it. None. I was on autopilot. They didn't fire me, so it couldn't have been too awful. A couple hours later I did the second show. Again, no memory whatsoever. It must've worked.

The next day my stuff arrived. My costume took a thousand-dollar downgrade, my guitar was a thousand-dollar upgrade, and the shows went well.

The next day the stagehand came up to me and said, "You've got to come outside."

"Why?" I asked.

"Because," he said, "Ann Margret never puts the opening act on the marquee. Never. Now let's go look."

We went out, and there on the huge marquee was Ann Margret and underneath, my name. Yes! I hadn't bombed! I was a Vegas act!

A couple more things. I went to a some after show parties at her suite, and they consisted of her and the cast drinking, talking and watching dance videos. I fit right in. You bet. I can't dance, I couldn't think of things to say, so I just sat quietly and tried not to drink too much and turn into John Wayne.

Maybe a month later I got booked on the TV Show, 'Live at the Improv," in L.A. In the afternoon before the show, the director, who had no clue who I was, asked me for some credits he could use when they introduced me. I'm sure he thought I was going to say something like, well, I just played Boise, Idaho, and Cheyenne, Wyoming, which would've been true a couple months before. This time I was able to say, "Well, I just opened for Ann Margret at Caesar's in Las Vegas." His eyes grew wide. I was no dirtbag entertainer. My status went way up.

I didn't mention I'd bombed on Johnny Carson. I figured it was none of his business.

Mike Neun

GOLF AND DYSFUNCTIONAL FAMILIES. FUN!

Where am I now?

In Chiangmai, Thailand, with my wife sitting across the bedroom watching Netflix videos. I love this life. Outside, a monk spoke for a long time on a loudspeaker at a funeral down the road.

This morning I played golf with New Orleans Joe at the crack of dawn. I have dreams of starting the Dawn Patrol Golf League. Fast golfers go first, no handicap system, just make your own bets. If someone's a sandbagger, simple, don't play him. Once word gets out he'll be a lonely golfer.

About five years ago I met a guy at Chiangmai Highlands Golf Course named Tony. He's an ex-police chief from California, and he's the one who turned me on to early morning golf. He would tee off in the dark just to get on the course first and we played lots of rounds together.

Tony is a big, cheerful Italian guy who says hello to everyone. All the workers on the course know him, all the caddies know him, and we had good times. We also took a trip to DaNang, Vietnam, with Derek to play golf and had a great time.

I think he was also a fine, honest policeman and chief. He talked of times officials tried to get him to fix tickets and he showed them the door. He also talked about domestic disturbance calls and how dangerous they were. Remember, he was a cop during the Vietnam protests and the days of police being called pigs. We came from wildly different perspectives on all that so the conversations were interesting, but we found common ground in our distrust of organized religion.

After a couple of years I told him I wanted to play some rounds on my own and work on my game. I must've said it wrong because that was the last we played together. Social skills? No thank you, I prefer to drive people away. We did meet for coffee occasionally and had long conversations but sadly, he's back in the U.S. now battling lung cancer.

I did thank him many times for getting me to play early morning golf, which pretty much saved me. In the league that started at noon I couldn't figure out why I wasn't enjoying the games. I couldn't understand why I'd get angry after 13 or 14 holes and turn into a raving asshole. Now I know I was hot, exhausted, and close to sun stroke. I'm not kidding. One time I came home from a round and couldn't remember the names of the people around me. I had to take a cold shower and a nap to get back to normal.

The good news is I never got angry at my caddy. Over here, some golfers treat the caddies badly and I have walked off the course rather than play with them.

So this morning was another great day on the course. Then off to Danisa's for another traditional Thai breakfast. Joe had a pulled-pork and jalapino sandwich and I had a falafel wrap. I should point out that I love Thai food and eat it all the time.

After breakfast I took a short nap and went for a haircut. I picked a salon at random and the lady was wearing jeans

Mike Neun

shorts and a tee-shirt, showing some tattoos. A spider web on her elbow, a spider on her forearm, a pyramid of Thai letters on the back of her neck which looked like a Buddhist thing, and she seemed nice. I always have the feeling barbers and stylists aren't that enthused about talking, especially if they're Thai and I'm not. But that might be me projecting. If I were a stylist, I'd want to concentrate on cutting hair, not on carrying on a conversation screwed up by a language barrier.

To set her mind at ease I pulled out my cell phone and read a book while she worked. It was peaceful, except for the book, which featured a pipe bomb, three deaths, a fight under water, and an escape. Yes, I do read mysteries. The haircut went well but there was no shampoo before or after. This is unusual in Thailand and I have come to enjoy the shampoos. Usually they're done by an apprentice stylist and are more like a head massage. This bare bones haircut cost 120 baht—four dollars. I love Thailand. When I got home my wife's mom thought the haircut looked stupid. The kids agreed. Oh well, it'll grow out.

As I said earlier, my first musical instrument was a ukulele and I do not know where it came from. No, wait, at first I took piano lessons. Both Mom and Dad could play classical piano and my dad could play some rag time. So they got me a teacher and I hated the lessons. They saw the writing on the wall and let me quit. I must've been in grade school when I got the ukulele and I dreamed of being a big star. We lived in Michigan and we used to take vacations in Southhampton, Ontario. There was a resort there, and I think we went there two or three summers in a row. This time I had the ukulele and I would sit in the corner playing it, hoping someone would ask me to play and I'd be the life of the party.

Nothing happened until one night there were a lot of people in one of the dining rooms and someone wondered what they should do. My sister, Nancy, piped up, "Mike can play the ukulele!"

So I picked up my instrument, played brilliantly, a talent scout happened to be there and I was signed to a huge contract with Columbia records. Wrong.

What really happened was that I jumped up and ran out of the room and down the beach crying. The pressure was too much and I was too shy. Not the greatest start to a show business career.

I should tell you about my sister, Nancy. And I should also say that a book about her would be amazing. I only wish I knew more about her life, because I've heard all kinds of tales. We just never lived in the same places after we left home. Here's what I know:

Nan was my little sister and we played together when we were kids. My most vivid memory was at a swimming pool, where she tried some dive off the low board and hit her head on the side of the pool. I thought she was dead and my parents rushed to her but she got up. It was very scary but she was all right.

Her best friend in high school was Camille Osario, who later married a friend of mine, Tom Tilley. Their daughter was a teacher in California who went to jail on a weird charge of romancing a student, and Camille and Tom have spent the rest of their lives fighting not just for their daughter, but for the rights of the accused. Life is weird.

Nancy went to college at the University of Washington and became a sorority girl. At the UW, every year the fraternities would select queens and then there'd be a queen of queens and my sister, who I didn't realize people thought was beautiful, became the queen of queens at this university of 17,000 people. Then she dropped out, went down to Haight Ashbury in San Francisco, and became a flower child. Ours is not a normal family.

I think she went down there with Billie Roberts, a folksinger I'd met in Seattle. He came into town in a hippie VW van with the most beautiful woman I'd ever seen and dazzled us all with his blues guitar and harmonica. Upon seeing that girl, I immediately bought a harmonica (or "harp" as Billie would say) and he taught me how to play blues by breathing in and bending notes. I then spent years on the road, driving through all the states in the northwest practicing blues harp while I drove, one hand for the wheel, one hand for the harp. Billie was a fine guitar player and singer, but his main claim to fame was writing the song, "Hey Joe", which Jimi Hendrix made famous.

I know very little of Nancy's life in California. I do know she was a waitress at the bar where Carole Doda became hugely famous as a go-go dancer with large breast implants. Nan told me years later that when Carole left, they wanted Nancy to get breast implants and replace her. She declined.

She had all kinds of friends. She slightly knew Alden Kelly, an ex-Hell's Angel who made the Grateful Dead album cover with a skeleton and roses.

But she did get heavily involved in drugs and liquor and Billy tried to get her out of that life. I knew none of this, as I was up in the Northwest singing in bars. Our parents were so proud.

What I do know is that one day (or night, I can't remember) Nan was on the back of a borrowed Suzuki 600 motorcycle being driven by long-haired guy who sold vacuum cleaners door to door. A Cadillac blew through a stop sign and T-boned them. Nan was badly injured with a broken pelvis. I went down to see her, along with our parents, and it was really sad but she was upbeat.

She recovered, and overcame drugs and alcohol. This alone makes her a hero in my eyes. She also had a daughter,

Onami, and they got out of San Francisco and moved to Ohio. I have no idea why, but she's lived there ever since. She's worked various low-paying jobs and happily lives a hippie life. She's also come to visit us in Chiangmai, and she seems both fragile and strong. We email each other about our various bouts with depression, and life in general, and I am proud to be her brother.

One more thing. Our mother. Mom and Dad were very smart and graduated near the top of their classes at Wayne University in Detroit. They were also talented, both playing the piano and active in amateur theaters in Michigan. My theory is that Mom should've had a career. I don't think she was cut out to be a housewife, but I normally don't have a clue about other people so you can take that with a grain of salt. Both Mom and Dad were very attractive and very social, with lots of friends and lots of gatherings at our house.

We three kids were a huge disappointment to Mom.

I should include our younger brother, Tim. He was a surprise baby, arriving seven years after Nancy. Tim is a great guy and we've been quite close over the years. His first problem was that he was chubby as a kid. He was a good pitcher in little league, but got razzed unmercifully about his weight. He also didn't like school much, which was a big letdown to Mom and Dad.

In high school he developed a love of pottery and spent hours in his downstairs bedroom throwing pots on his wheel. He became quite good. All I know is one night he got in a huge argument with Mom and broke all his pots. I have no idea what that was about, as I was away at college and heard about it later.

He made it out of high school and tried college but didn't like it. What he did like was skiing. Mom had forced him to go skiing. He fought it, didn't want to go, but then he fell in love with it. He told me how the kids used to make jumps under the chairlift so they could show off, and one time he jumped too close to the lift tower. You know those metal loops they use as rungs to climb the lift towers? He got about ten feet in the air and the tip of his ski went through that loop and it ripped off the ski. All he could remember was the collective gasp of the people on the chairs above, but he landed the jump on one ski and got a huge round of applause. Of course he then had to take off the ski, climb the tower and get his other ski, which was kind of anticlimactic.

Tim quit college and boom, got drafted. By then the Vietnam protests were going strong and people were questioning the war. Tim thought the war was wrong and with the help of Quakers, refused to go. He didn't bail out to Canada, he just said no, I won't go. They put him in prison for six months, at a minimum security prison in Oregon where they planted trees. It doesn't sound too bad but it was still prison and one of the other inmates was nicknamed "Walking Death." Scary.

A few years before I'd spent two years in the army. At the time I thought it was the right thing to do. But as time went on, and I met people who'd actually been in Vietnam, I came to realize how wrong that war was. I also have to admit I might've been the last person to figure that out. So there I was, an ex-soldier with a brother who was a draft resistor.

I was so proud of him. He was dead right. Tim is the kind of guy who makes up his mind and that's it. He won't back down. And he won't go sideways. I'm not sure, if I'd had that choice, that I would've faced prison with that kind of courage.

When he got out, I was living in Ketchum when I wasn't on the road, and skiing at Sun Valley. He had to go on probation and work a public service job, so I helped get him a janitor's job at the Sun Valley Hospital.

Tim wrote me his recollection of that process:

> *The guy that hired me at the hospital was named Ackerman—I'm glad I remember shit like that but struggle with my kids' names! Somehow you met him—probably through the Ram Bar—because you must have told him that I needed a job "in the interest of the nation" and he hired me right on the spot, then, a few days later he interviewed me. I told him my choices were to be the best janitor they ever had or I got to go back to prison. He cracked up and I started the next day. I also remember my probation officer drove up from Boise for a surprise visit. He came by the house and was appalled that I was living with Bev and had bought a house. That's against the rules! Then he went to the hospital & talked to Ackerman who must have given me a pretty good recommendation. I went to work and he was there and said he better not hear anything about me. He didn't and I never saw or heard from him again.*

Tim would work at night and ski all day, probably not what the probation people had in mind. Mount Baldy was the ski mountain and some days I would look up and see tracks way off the groomed runs, through trees and places no one else had gone. I knew they were Tim's. He was never a racer, he hated moguls, but he was a wild back-country skier.

He later got a job in a ski shop and he and his friends would goof around with the skis, putting the mountings up towards the toe or way back just to see what they'd do. They'd also laminate weird stuff on top and I became the first skier up there to have plaid skis.

Tim later became a woodworker and furniture maker and taught woodworking at the University of Oregon. He's married

Mike Neun

to Cindy, a midwife who later became a hospital administrator and they live in Eugene, Oregon. He still is a great skier.

So my poor mom ended up with me, a college graduate who chucked it all to go sing in sleazy bars, Nan, who ran off to be a drug-addled flower child with a baby out of wedlock, and Tim, a draft resistor who went to prison. Mom was not a happy camper, and I think it messed her up.

Nan used to get letters from Mom, and she'd have friends read them first so they could take out the crazy parts.

Dad? I think he got caught in the middle of all this. He was a businessman, and a good one. When he retired, he kept un-retiring and going back into business. I think Mom was hard to live with. But she was also way ahead of her time when it came to women's rights and championing the underdog. As with all of us, a mixed bag.

Dad kept surprising me.

One day, late in his life, he turned to me and said, "I never wanted to be a businessman. I wanted to be an actor, but we got out of school in the middle of the Depression. There weren't a lot of choices."

Another time, and I should preface this by saying our family attended church regularly when we were kids, he turned to me and said, "You know, I've always been an atheist."

My immediate response was, "Why the hell did we have to go to church all those years?"

He said it just was what people did back then.

One final story.

Until I think of other final stories.

When I was part of a duo, singing in bars with Brian, we got booked to play five Playboy Clubs. One was the Jamaica Playboy Club in Ocho Rios and it was a glorious gig with a great showroom, good sound and lights, beautiful beaches out front, and resort accommodations. And yes, there were Playboy bunnies serving drinks.

You know what else was great, and I'd never seen it in any club before or since? Each table had a card on it that said, "As a courtesy to the other patrons, please refrain from talking during the performances." How cool is that???

One of the bunnies was named Nancy and she was a registered nurse from Philadelphia. She was quite beautiful. Well, we got together. This was a bit of a shock to the club's sports director who thought he had the inside track, and one night on the beach we saw him stalking us. Weird.

Our affair was wildly romantic—swimming at night, hanging out in Jamaica—and at the end of our gig I gave her money for a plane ticket to Atlantic City, our next club. I have to admit I didn't know if she'd actually take me up on it, but she did. She quit her job and joined me in Atlantic City and we traveled together for about six months.

Ah! But here's the life lesson. In those days, to my mom, Playboy Magazine was the work of the devil and the Playboy Clubs were scandalous places. She seemed to vacillate between being a liberated woman and a religious fanatic. The lesson is, if Mom's in her righteous phase, don't bring a Playboy bunny home to meet the folks. Silly me, I thought the visit went well and Nancy was a great, intelligent person and a nurse, and things seemed okay.

My superpower is obliviousness.

My dad told me later that Mom went off like Mount Vesuvius. As soon as we were gone, she exploded and he caught the brunt of it.

Boom!

Nancy the nurse-bunny? A friend of mind saw her a couple of years later at a tailgate party at a Lakers game in L.A. She'd married a doctor and seemed very happy. Good for her.

Mike Neun

So there you have it. I guess we were a dysfunctional family, whatever that is. But I love my brother and sister, and they are a great part of my life. I also loved my mom and dad. They did so much for us, and I also now realize how hard it is to be a parent. I think Mom went off the deep end, and wine might've been involved, or menopause, but those days are gone now.

I wish Tim and Nan would write books because they'd probably enlighten me on what really went on. As I say, obliviousness is my superpower.

Ah! One last story about Mom. She and I fought constantly, mostly about what a disappointment I was and how I'd let them down and how could I go sing in bars, and how I was ungrateful, and so on. One day, while I was out on the road, I wrote her a letter saying that we were just making each other really sad and maybe we should take some time off. Maybe not communicate for a year or two until we could be calm and civilized with each other. I thought it was a well-reasoned compromise, and mailed it off.

Okay, I'm not good at some things. One of them is dates—anniversaries, holidays, birthdays, and so on. I swear I had no idea Mother's Day was coming up. Really. Well, that's when the letter arrived. Again, Vesuvius. My poor father.

YO HO HO AND
A CAN OF VARNISH

In Seattle, in the '70s, I had a friend named Wind Whitehall. He came to a couple of my shows and we got talking and became buddies. He lived on a 56-foot wooden schooner in Puget Sound. I had never been a boat person, but he took me sailing and I liked it. As usual, I was doing things backwards. Most people learn to sail in dinghies and work up. I started on a large schooner and worked down.

Wind was a carpenter who did extremely fine work, but had no sense of time. He would start a job, get distracted, and finish a few weeks after he said he would, which resulted in some pissed-off customers. He wasn't very successful, but he taught me a lot about sailing and about working on wooden boats. I like working with wood, and sailboats are the ultimate test because there are no right angles. Everything is curved, or a compound curve, and it really is a test of skill. So I would help him and he would take me sailing. We sailed up to the wooden boat festival in Victoria, Canada, and I was knocked out by the beauty of the boats and how nice the people were. In no time, Wind had talked me into buying a boat.

We found a 37-foot sloop named Watauga and I bought it from a family of genuine salt-water sailors. They'd sailed it to Hawaii and back and it was a really sea-worthy boat. It was designed by Ed Monk, and built in 1938 out of Port Orford cedar, with teak decks and cabin, and a spruce mast. It was a beautiful, sound, sailboat. I was a novice sailor, planning to live aboard.

We had a marine surveyor inspect the boat at a shipyard in Lake Union. He could find no major problems, so I bought the boat. They put it back in the water and Wind and I sailed it over to the Ballard Locks to take it out into Puget Sound. The Ballard Locks are kind of a tourist attraction, with people standing around watching the boats go in, the water lowering or rising, and the boats going out the other end. We motored into the lock behind a giant tugboat, and I shifted into reverse to bring my boat to a stop. There was no reverse. Oops. Meanwhile, the tugboat had drifted from the wall and we were coasting in between it and the wall, which was not a good place to be. Crushing my boat was a distinct possibility. Wind was quick, and he yelled up to the lock keepers and soon every line they had was thrown down to us. We grabbed them, they hauled us back just in time and the tourists got a thrill. It was the beginning of me realizing my skills were minimal and boats could malfunction at any time.

All I remember now are vignettes.

The best one is when Kelly, my second wife, and I were sailing in Puget Sound in light breezes. This meant we were going about two knots and eating cheese and crackers. I have no idea what we were talking about, but somehow Kelly came out with the line, "Happy hour is the saddest part of the day." I got excited. It had to be one of the great country western song titles. I wrote some lyrics and a friend of ours, Bruce Innes, wrote the music.

Mike Neun

John Powell was my manager and he sold it to Ray Stevens, the country singer. We split the royalties three ways after a commission to John.

We all made money, but Bruce got the idea I was cheating him. He wrote me a nasty letter, claiming he wasn't getting his share of the mechanicals. I had no idea what mechanicals even were. I just got checks and split the money up. The letter really bothered me, so I loaded all my royalty records into my Austin-Healey and drove 12-hours from Portland to Ketchum, Idaho, where Bruce was living. I got there, opened the trunk filled with file folders, and told him he could go through all of them. He said he didn't think that was necessary and he was sorry about the letter. He was also upset that his name wasn't on the record credits and I agreed. He and Kelly should've been listed as co-writers. We called BMI to try to change that. We weren't successful, but I told him I'd do anything he could think of to change it. I thought we parted as friends, but something had soured our relationship. I hated that, because he was one of the most talented guys I ever knew. He played great blues guitar and piano, sang really well, wrote great songs and had a wicked sense of humor. He sang all kinds of songs but my two favorites were "Momma's in the Sky with Elvis" and "Bad Dancing, Look at them White Folks Go."

Back to the boat.

I first docked it at Shilshole Bay Marina in Seattle and Wind and I sailed it around Puget Sound. I got so I could single-hand it, but I was a bit leery about big storms. I'd started doing shows on cruise ships, and one of my first cruises was on Holland America. The ship got into a storm and I stood on the 12th deck forward watching the bow crash into 30-foot waves and feeling the spray hit me, 12 stories above the water. I tried to picture myself in my 37-foot sloop slamming into those waves and realized I was probably not an ocean sailor.

Two boats away from me in the marina was a couple who'd sailed around the world and I was in awe. I've read lots of sailing books, filled with people throwing out storm anchors and tying themselves to the boat, or rolling in giant waves and getting dismasted. I also read about one couple going around the Cape of Good Hope whose sailboat went end over end in a giant wave. She broke her leg, but they survived. To me, this didn't sound like fun.

I realized that my idea of thrill-seeking is reading books about thrill seekers. I am not an adrenalin junky. Walking out on stage was scary enough for me and I was amazed at the sailing stories my friends told me.

About a year later I moved the boat to Eagle Harbor on Bainbridge Island, across from Seattle. There I met Dean and Kopi Carmine who were true ocean sailors. They'd bought a 27-foot lake boat because that was all they could afford and Dean reinforced the fiberglass hull and all the fittings so they could go ocean sailing. They took it from Seattle down to the Marquesas Islands in the South Pacific and then up to Hawaii and back to Seattle. All this in a 27-foot lake boat. Damn.

Dean is one of those guys who knows a lot about everything and is great at working on boats, so he can get a job anywhere in the world.

We had another guy in the marina who'd sailed his boat to Hawaii and back single-handed, and one night he set the boat on auto pilot and went below to get an hour or two of sleep. He awoke to find his boat scraping along the hull of a giant container ship. Somehow, his boat survived and he made it to port.

My adventures were way smaller.

One day I learned that emergencies never come alone. If something is going to go wrong, other things will go wrong at the same time. We were motoring and we

Mike Neun

smelled smoke. The control panel was on fire. Luckily I got to the fire extinguisher before it spread, but two other things went wrong at the same time. I can't remember what they were, because I'm old and it was 40 years ago. I think we were taking on water through the stuffing box or something. Anyway, we survived.

Another time we ran aground, which sounds like a big deal but it wasn't. It was another light breeze day on Puget Sound and we got too close to shore. We were just drifting with the sails flapping and suddenly we just stopped. If you're going to run aground, that's the only way to go. Luckily we were on a rising tide and a half hour later I was able to motor off.

The most dangerous adventure was one time I was sailing back from the San Juan Islands with a young couple on vacation. We were sailing across the Straights of Juan de Fuca which separates Puget Sound from Canada. The wind was blowing against the tide, so it was choppy and slow and I was tired. I was aiming for a channel between Port Townsend and Whidbey Island but didn't realize the tide was pushing us toward the island. A fishing boat came out from Port Townsend and motored toward me and circled. I thought that's strange, so I took a look around an realized I was way to close to shore. I flipped on the depth finder and I was in 15 feet of water over a rocky bottom and my boat had a 6-foot keel. I started the diesel and motored the hell out of there, thanking God for that fishing boat.

You always remember the wild times, but there were lots of good times with friends on board, sailing around Puget Sound. And I learned too that boat people are the best. If you ever have a problem, someone in the marina will know how to solve it and will help you. If you're at sea and have a problem, people in other boats will come to your aid.

Later on I met Kelly and she moved aboard with me. It takes a special kind of woman to live aboard a 37-foot boat with no kitchen and the bathroom and shower a long walk up the dock. Kelly was 5 foot 7 and I'm 6 feet tall, and I think we both developed permanent stoops from the lack of headroom. But it was romantic too, and the beautiful thing about a boat is if you don't like your neighbors you just untie it and move somewhere else. Also the gentle slapping of halyards on masts can be a peaceful way to drift off to sleep.

Up from the dock was the Pegassus Coffeehouse, run by our friend Dave Dessinger. It was perfect for morning coffee and I also did some little shows up there. We had great people to hang out with, we learned a lot about sailing and boats, and I developed great skills with sanding, varnishing, woodwork and painting.

And lastly was the time I had the boat hauled out in Lake Union for the annual painting of the hull and bottom. I worked for a week and when we put the boat back in the water it looked truly beautiful. The hull was blindingly white, the varnish shone on the teak cabin, it was a boat to be proud of. It was Sunday, and I got through the Ballard Locks without incident, sailed across Puget Sound, and pulled into Eagle Harbor Marina. People were out on their boats, visiting, having drinks, and I proudly sailed in, lowered the sails perfectly, started the motor, turned into the marina, turned into my slip, shifted into reverse and again, there was no reverse. This was the new gearbox I'd had installed when the last one failed. I think we're talking design flaw here.

I was headed toward the dock with no way to stop. Luckily the dock was low, and the bow just climbed up over it, but then it just hung there. It wouldn't slide back into the water. All over the marina, people applauded. "Nice landing!" "You don't even have to tie up!"

Humbling.

Mike Neun

Epilogue:

Eventually we sold the boat, and it was a sad day. We lost money on it, because boats aren't like houses, they're like cars. They depreciate. We sold it to some friends, but they didn't have the money to keep it up. A few years later I went back to Bainbridge Island and saw Watauga, my beautiful wooden boat, blocked up in a field. It was covered with a mildewed tarp and the hull was moldy streaked with dirt. I knew it would never sail again. Damn.

Epilogue Two:

In the bridge club here in Chiangmai I met Mike Williams who moved here from Whidbey Island near Seattle. Yes, that Whidbey Island where I almost put my boat on the rocks. It turns out he was a sailor too. When he graduated from the University of Washington, he and his friends bought a 50-foot schooner and sailed it around the world. My little adventures pale in comparison. He wrote a book about it, called *The Chronicles of the Schooner Lusty 1* and it's a great read.

Epilogue Three:

I learned the true power of the ocean on a Seabourn cruise ship east of Greenland. Usually cruise ships are very good at avoiding storms but now and then one changes path and the ship has to deal with it.

The old Seabourn ships, the Pride and the Spirit, were very small cruise ships and I can't remember which one I was on, but we hit that storm and it was a big one. The ship was handling it well, with the captain angling into 30-foot waves, and everyone on board was hanging on to something. You know what is really dangerous on a cruise ship? Pianos. Pianos are huge, heavy, and if they start rolling around a dance floor they can be lethal. Ours were chained down always, so that was not a problem. You know the term "loose cannon?" It's the same thing. On the old fighting ships, if a cannon broke loose in a storm it could roll around the decks and kill people.

On this ship, up in the bow was a water-tight door leading from the deck into the cabin area. Water-tight doors are those heavy steel doors that you lock by turning a large wheel which inserts heavy steel bars into the bulkhead of the ship. Those doors are very, very strong. Well, a huge wave crashed into that door and bent it. I didn't believe that was possible. So now there was an opening and the ship was taking on water through that opening.

Our Norwegian captain got on the loudspeaker and explained the problem. He warned us he was going to have to turn the ship around so the stern faced the waves and the crew could weld a patch on the water-tight door. It was a really tricky maneuver, where he waited till the ship climbed up the face of a wave and then he cranked it hard and gave it full power to make the turn on top of the wave. It was a superb piece of seamanship and once on the new course the crew was able to repair the door. Then he had to duplicate the turn to get us back going into the waves—the safest course for a ship in a storm.

There are amateur sailors like me, and then there are seamen. I am well aware of the difference.

Mike Neun

COMEDIAN FACES BEARS AND LIVES TO TELL ABOUT IT

I was playing the lounge at the Antler's Plaza Hotel in Colorado Springs and it wasn't going well. I was trying desperately to become more than a barroom entertainer by introducing original, subtle material into my shows. Guess what. People drinking in bars aren't clamoring for original, subtle material. They want to bust loose and have a good time. So I was struggling.

One morning after a particularly bad night I decided to get a good book, take it out into the woods, and spend the day reading in peace. I bought a Horatio Hornblower novel, always a good choice, got in my car and headed out of town into the forests of Colorado. I parked at a campground, grabbed my book and headed into the woods. I walked for quite awhile, found a good tree to lean against, and sat down to read my sea-going adventure. It was peaceful. I was immersed in the Hornblower escapades. Perfect.

That's when I heard shots.

They were off in the distance but I suddenly remembered a couple of guys in the bar talking about the start of hunting season and realized this was it. Well, crap. There I was in my brown jacket, with long brown hair, and people were looking for deer to shoot. I sprang to my feet and ran back to the campground.

There was a little hill just before the campground and I came charging over it and then went into cartoon mode. You know where the character is running, sees something scary and his legs go into reverse while he's still moving forward? That was me. In the campground near my car was a garbage can and surrounding it were three bears. They were every bit as startled as I was and by the time I stopped we all stood frozen, the bears, startled, on their hind legs staring at me and me, in terror, staring at them.

I then repeated my bear zen mantra, "Oh shit, shit, shit, shit...." and edged ever so slowly to the car, trying to get it between me and the bears. I finally made it, somehow got the key in the lock, opened it, jumped inside and slammed the door shut. I then sat there and repeated my mantra about fifty more times as I waited for my body to stop shaking. Eventually I was able to drive back to the Antler's Plaza. That night I went back into cheerful, loud, barroom entertainment mode and did better. I finished the Hornblower novel in my room, bear free.

Mike Neun

JINTANA,
THE LOVE OF MY LIFE

I first came to Thailand on a cruise ship in the 1980s. It was the Royal Viking Star, and we docked in Sattahip. The passengers went on tours up to Bangkok and the crew and entertainers headed for Pattaya. Pattaya at the time made Sodom and Gomorrah look like church camp. You could go to a different girly bar every night for three years and never repeat. You could find every perversion imaginable.

We got there at a time when the U.S. fleet was in town. Ten thousand sailors and every bargirl in Southeast Asia. Awesome!

We took songtaws into town. They are red pickup trucks fitted with two bench seats in the back and a cover over the top.

It was 40 years ago and I don't remember much. There was a lot of nakedness on stage. Thai people laugh a lot, even while performing lewd acts in front of drunken idiots. There was audience participation. Take any U.S. strip club you've ever seen and multiply it by ten.

I, of course, was morally outraged. "This is wrong!" I said, as we got really drunk and went from bar to bar. "God will punish you!" I thought as an audience applauded the finish of a hand job in the back of the room. "I could retire here!" as we staggered back to the ship.

Well, I was right. I did retire to Thailand and I first went to Pattaya to meet a golfer friend. There are lots of good golf courses in that area and we played them all, but I soon realized even I was not sleazy enough to live in Pattaya. So I moved to Chiangmai.

I played golf. I went to bars. I hung out with friends. I lived in a cheap apartment and bought a used Honda Civic. I didn't want some Thai girl to think I was rich and hustle me for my money. It worked. No Thai women hustled me and I thought, oops, maybe I've made a mistake. It would've been nice to be hustled. Oh sure, if I walked down Loi Kroh road past the girly bars I could hear women call out, "Hey, young handsome man." This was always morale building but I had a suspicion it wasn't true.

I lived in a place called Chaimansion, which was not a mansion. It was a small apartment building but the apartments did have high ceilings, which is a rarity in Thailand. I paid 10,000 baht (about 330 dollars) a month for a one-room apartment, plus bath, and it was fine for me because I've lived a life in hotel rooms.

In one of the other apartments was an English guy named Lee, and he had a girlfriend. She worked at Payap University and she had a girlfriend who also worked there. Lee asked if I wanted to meet that lady. I said yes, but I wasn't looking for a deep relationship or marriage because I'd proven I was really lousy at both. I just wanted someone to hang out with. Also, I said, I know this is dead wrong and a bad thing to say, but I don't want to go with a fat woman.

I can hear people screaming as they read this, and they are right. You should love someone for their intelligence, their inner beauty, and all their other qualities. A good person would do this and obviously, I fell way short. I love to eat but

Mike Neun

I balanced that by being a jogger for 35 years, and I wanted a woman who liked to exercise and stay healthy.

Also I'd seen women talk about the bait and switch move, where they get slim, find a guy, marry him and say, "Okay! I can eat!" Six months later they've gained 30 pounds and the guy is wondering what the hell happened. Obviously it goes both ways. A woman marries a handsome dude and he becomes a couch potato with a 30-pound beer gut. Should she stay?

Lee assured me she wasn't fat and I assured him I wasn't a horrible, bigoted person but it rang a bit hollow because I'd just proved I was. He set it up.

For our blind date we made plans to go to dinner, the four of us, and I picked up Jintana at the Airport Plaza Mall. My first sight of her was coming down the stairs from the mall and my first memory was that she had the greatest smile I'd ever seen. She was small, just under 5-feet tall, with short black hair and a beautiful face.

When she got in the car I had the band "Blue" playing on the CD player and she told me later she was surprised a guy my age would listen to that music. I didn't tell her I'd spent the last 20 years working cruise ships and was suffering from Andrew Lloyd Webber PTSD. Since coming to Thailand I'd listened to nothing but hip hop, rock, grunge—anything but themes from musicals. By the way, I think one of the best band names in the world is a Bangkok band called, "Thaitanium."

We drove to a restaurant on Canal Road and I realized she spoke English really well, with a beautiful Thai accent. At dinner I was entranced.

The upshot was that we started going together and one afternoon, in my cheap apartment, we made love and it was glorious. After that, I would pick her up at the University, bring her back to the apartment where we'd spend time together, and then take her home because her parents were strict about her not staying over at my place. I found this a bit over protective because she was 36 at the time.

Then the dreaded "M" word came up, and I explained that I was way too old for her, that I'd been married twice before and they were dismal failures, and that it would be a terrible choice for her. Six months later, we got married.

That was 13 years ago and they've been the best 13 years of my life. Jintana, like most Thai women, is a very strong person. I'll never forget one thing she said very early on. "If you're looking for a typical subservient Thai woman, you're a generation too late."

The other awesome thing about this relationship is Jintana's family. We eventually moved into the family home and lived with Jintana's mom, her sister and brother-in-law, two nieces, and Bo the housekeeper. I realized this family really had it together. I'd never seen such a balance between love and discipline, and the two nieces are by far the best kids I've ever been around. They are bright, cheerful, good students, and have great senses of humor. Oh sure, in the early years when I drove them to school, they tended to sing, "Itsy Bitsy Spider" endlessly because they knew it bugged me, but we had great fun.

About four years ago, Jintana's sister built a house 15 feet away from ours and now their family lives next door while Jintana, her mom and I rattle around in the big family home. But the kids still hang out with us and I still drive them to school.

Jintana's father was a hard-working man who loved his children. Their family story is a really, really good one.

Jintana's mom grew in the Omkoi district, in Chiangmai province but deep in the hills south of Chiangmai city. She was raised in a tiny village and her dad (Jintana's grandfather) owned elephants and had lots of people working for him in

Mike Neun

the jungle. When Jintana's mom was about 12 the family moved down from the village, past Chiangmai to the town of Fang. They put their belongings on elephants and her mom rode horseback while others walked or rode. The trip took a week.

Jintana's mom, Chan Ploy, lived in Fang and it was there she met Jintana's dad, Suwan, a farmer. They fell in love but didn't marry. Chan Ploy, when she was 22, tried to move back to her village with her cousins. Suwan, persistent, decided to follow her there. Chan Ploy's mom sent word she wanted her daughter to come back to Fang, and on her way back she met Suwan, coming up to find her. How romantic is that?

They made the trek back to Fang and Suwan and Chan Ploy got married. We have pictures of them when they were young and she was quite beautiful and he was quite handsome. Jintana and Maew, her older sister, were born in their house in Fang with a midwife delivering them.

When Jintana was 2 years old, her family moved to Chiangmai and the youngest sister, Tai, was born in the only government hospital there. Jintana's dad was a photographer, a barber, dispensed medicine and shots for men with sexual diseases, raised pigs and ducks and basically worked very, very hard. Chan Ploy was a housewife and managed the small amounts of money Suwan was able to bring in. Together they put all three girls through school and university. Maew and Tai graduated from Payap University, a private institution, while Jintana graduated from Chiangmai University, a government school. It's an amazing success story.

Jintana's younger sister, Tai, is now a bank manager. Her older sister, Maew, is married to a Danish man and living in Copenhagen where she works in a nursing home and he works at a bread company.

Sadly, Jintana's father died twelve years ago from lung cancer. Jintana and her sisters are sad they never got a chance to show him the world and spend more time with him. I barely got to know him, but I have to think he was a really fine father.

Jintana is 49 now and as beautiful and funny as ever. We live a quiet life, as we both like to read and spend time with the kids.

About five years ago we took her mom to the hospital and it looked like she was near death. They had her in ICU, and the doctor prepared the family for her passing. Yeah, right. That was five years ago and her mom made an amazing recovery and is still going strong. She's got lots of health problems, and doesn't get around much, but she's hanging in there.

When we go out with my friends, Jintana always impresses them mightily. She's intelligent, quick-witted, speaks English fluently, and is quite beautiful. People wonder how I got so lucky, and I tell them it's my vast wealth and movie star looks. Jintana rolls her eyes.

Finally, she has always treated me with great kindness and warmth. I never believed a marriage could be like this, and I will be forever grateful and forever in love.

Mike Neun

HIT THE ROAD, THAI STYLE

L et me tell you about Thai traveling.

It's not like our family did it, where the kids are in the back seat whining, "When are we going to get there?" It's not about finding the fastest route and planning things. For Thai people, the trip itself is an adventure, and what would take me 5 hours will take them 8 or 10 hours easily. And they will have about 80% more fun.

First, every family has a cousin with a van. You pile in and head out of town, but if you see anything interesting along the way, you stop. Roadside stands are always favorites, and the women have to check out the different produce. Then there's food. Thai people love to eat, and they do it much better than what I'm used to. There is no such thing as your food and my food. You stop at a restaurant, everyone orders, the food is put in the middle of the table and everyone eats whatever they want. I was always terrible at sharing my food and that is now out the window. It wasn't as though I had a choice. You either share, or people look at you like you're an idiot. I am now a better person when it comes to sharing food.

Also, if there's a tourist attraction, you have to stop. It's the law. Meanwhile, while you're in the van, there is lots of laughter, sleeping when you feel like it, snacking, and no complaining at all. It's an adventure.

I was on the road in the U.S. for 40 years and I had no idea travel could be this stress free. Oh sure, some Thai drivers are maniacal speed freaks and the only solution is to avoid them. On the other hand I've played golf with ex-pats who feel it's okay to down five or ten beers after the game and then climb behind the wheel. All nationalities have their idiots. I once saw a blind drunk Englishman stagger out of Number 1 Bar mumbling, "If I can find it, I can drive it." People tried to stop him, but he was big, drunk and belligerent. Insanity.

Part of the lack of Thai travel stress could be because Jintana and her family grew up really poor. A road trip was exciting, something to be treasured. Or maybe Thai people are more easy-going than Americans. Or maybe both.

I just realized I'm generalizing and that's a huge mistake. I'm sure there are dysfunctional Thai families here with angry parents and spoiled kids and the whole catastrophe. The good news is I've never been on a trip with them so I can keep my illusions.

Mike Neun

How Can Smokin' Aces
Lead You to Politics?

Today I started watching *Smokin' Aces* on Netflix. Wow, so much violence. I wanted an action flick, but this is like the movie version of *Caligula* on steroids. Way over the top. Stop the killing and torture!

Jintana just went to bed and is falling asleep three feet from me. We've turned on the air conditioning because winter is over and we didn't sleep well in the heat last night. There is no noise from the road below, where the last few nights were filled with funeral chanting and speeches, fireworks and a dog endlessly barking. It is quiet, except for the ringing in my right ear that never stops.

Politics? Did I hear you say you wanted to hear the political views of an ex-sixties commie pinko tree-hugging dope-smoking godless humanist save the whales hippie folksinger turned comedian? Of course you did, because there just aren't enough amateurs out there spewing insane political theories. Also, the climate in America is way too civilized and rational. People are too gentle, thoughtful and forgiving in our political discourse. Let's throw out some bombast and spread some hate!

Or not.

How's this for a premise? I know if you love President Trump I am not going to change your mind. Ever. I also know that if you're a liberal there's no need for me to say stuff you already agree with.

I also know I could easily be in a mountain cabin writing manifestoes because I'm really worried about my home country. I think we could lose democracy, free elections, justice for all, and government by and for the people. We could lose everything our forefathers fought for and that would be terribly sad.

Or...bright, young, compassionate Republicans and Democrats could rise up, clean up the corruption, restore justice, and lead a revival of all that is great in America. I have a rich fantasy life.

The good news is that the ideas won't die. Even if dictators rise up in every country on earth, the ideas of truth, justice, free press, free elections, compassion for the underdog—all the things that made democracy great—those ideas won't die. They will spring up somewhere and that scares dictators and dictator wannabes to death. The ideas are stronger than tyrants and they will bring down these evil bastards and posers. Their deaths won't be pretty and they will be reviled down through history. Dictators never figure this out. They never realize they're going to end up hanging from lamp posts or crumpled up dead in bunkers. If I had kids, I would tell them never to go into the dictator business.

MY DISASTROUS
FINANCIAL CRISIS

O kay, it's a big emergency.
        I FedExed my taxes last year and didn't feel good about the guy who waited on me. But then I thought, what could go wrong with FedEx?

I just got a notice from the IRS that they hadn't received my 2018 taxes. Damn!

So I tried the tracking number on the Internet. No result.

Then I blasted off a bunch of emails to my ex-hippie accountant in Eugene (do you see a trend here?) and no answer.

So now I'm remaining calm and handling this in a mature way, right? Nope. I'm freaking out. The IRS also showed the balance in my account and it's much lower than it should be.

So this will be a day of phoning the IRS, going to FedEx , trying to get in touch with my accountant, and picking up my passport from the visa agency, which is the one thing that has gone right in my dealings with governments.

I have no doubt there will be fines to pay and hoops to jump through and paperwork to deal with. This is not how retirement is supposed to be. I should be in a deck chair with a drink with a little umbrella in it, grossing out all the young people with my Speedo.

Then I think of Jintana's family, walking for a week into town to try to find a better life and realize my problems are not that big a deal. It will get worked out one way or another.

So now, off to start a new day in Chiangmai.

Okay, I may have overreacted. But the letter sounded ominous, like there were going to be fines or time in the slammer.

I handled it the way any paranoid idiot would handle it. I fired off more emails to my accountant, thinking she could send in the information faster. The next morning I went to the FedEx office and asked the nice lady to see if she could track it and she tried but didn't succeed and she pointed out it was sent in 2018 and it was at that point I realized I had the wrong receipt. Duh.

Yes, in my head I was accusing FedEx of stealing my taxes and cashing my cashier's check for $2,377 and now had to face the fact that I had the wrong receipt. Mumble mumble, I'm sorry, and I slunk out of the office. I can slink with the best of them.

I also went to the bank and had them trace the cashier's check to see if it had been cashed. The guy there was really nice and told me about some foreigner who just had to pay $6,000 in taxes, which was astonishing to him. We agreed that that foreigner had to be really rich. The bank guy couldn't get the information, so I went to the Indian place in the mall and had chicken tikka masala and garlic nan. The chicken tikka was tasty, but I was surprised to find you could make garlic nan that was tasteless. Must've been a secret recipe.

I went back to the bank and the guy said he'd have to call me later. He did, and the check had been cashed. Obviously by some thief, right? When I got back home I found the right

Mike Neun

receipt and I'd sent those taxes with DHL. Ahah! The dreaded DHL thief! Jintana called them and they searched and traced the package. It had been delivered to the Internal Revenue Department in Ogden, Utah.

That night we put 1,000 baht into Awee's phone, because I was going to call the IRS and the last time I did they announced there'd be an hour and a half wait to talk to someone. I was ready! I had games set up to play on the iPad, a comfortable chair, and the determination to sit through a long time on hold, listening to 300 announcements about how it is much easier to contact them online.

I called, and two minutes later I was talking to an IRS guy who was really nice. He asked about Thailand, apologized when he had me wait while he checked something, and didn't think the missing tax return was a big deal. He actually apologized to me because the check was cashed and the return misplaced. I didn't tell him about my illuminati DHL tax thief theory, because, hey, I'm not some sort of wacko.

He told me to just send in a copy of the return and not worry about it. It was a great relief.

The next day I got an email from Katie, my accountant, and she too felt it was no big deal. The IRS letter had also included the amount of money that was in my 2018 account and, as she was a professional, she added up my estimated tax payments and the cashier's check and it came out perfectly. I didn't tell her about my flat-earth, Sasquatch, Russian vote rigging, DHL master thief theory.

Today I sent in the copy of the return.

I'm not going to jail. There won't be thousands of dollars worth of fines. I haven't told Jintana most of this, because she already thinks I'm bordering on senility and I don't want her to take away the car keys.

Case closed.

THAILAND? ISN'T THAT SCARY?

First, I feel 30 times safer walking the streets of Chiangmai at night than I would feel in a city in the U.S. You can get in trouble here. If you say something disparaging about the Royal Family, you will end up behind bars. If you cause a Thai person to lose face, like in a road rage incident, he can legally shoot you. There are guns here, but I've never seen one. Oh wait, our brother-in-law is a policeman. He has one.

If you say the wrong thing to a drunk Thai or a drunk foreigner, you can get into a fight.

I once met a guy who ran a girly bar in Chiangmai and he told me this story. He'd just bought the bar, and one night a drunken foreigner came in and was causing trouble. The bar owner figured it was his job to get the drunk out of there so he started for him. But the girls stopped him. "No, boss, we'll handle this."

Then, to his bewilderment, they started taking off their shoes. What the hell? Then he tumbled to the method. Ever looked at bargirl shoes? Those glittery ones with the really high heels, some of them spiked, some of them clunky? Well, they make really scary weapons. The drunk saw them coming at him, shoes raised, and sobered up quickly. He turned around and was gone.

All that being said, my Canadian friend Jeff just got back from a golf outing in Chiang Rai and apparently they'd been sitting at a street bar after their golf game, about 5 p.m, having a beer. Suddenly there was a loud argument in the street between this tough, tattooed Danish guy and his Thai girlfriend and she was giving as good as she got. Then the guy, who was obviously on some mind-altering substance, came over to their table and said, "You guys laughing at this?"

Jeff and the others said no, they weren't laughing.

The guy then punched one of the golfers. A couple of times. And then was gone. The police got there after the action and arrested the girlfriend. The next day the golfers were called to the police station to give their statements and the Danish guy came in to get his girlfriend. He was wearing his biker colors and they found out he was the sergeant at arms in a notorious biker gang. Scary, because the sergeant at arms is usually the toughest guy in the gang of really tough guys. He threatened death to the golfers and the witnesses from the bar. But then the police showed him video of the incident. He didn't remember any of it. Apparently today's biker mind altering substances are a bit stronger than those drugs we had in the sixties. He apologized to them all, but the police took him up to immigration. Nobody knows what happened after that. He either got deported or he bought his way out of trouble. The golfers are pulling for the former.

I've been here 15 years and there is only one more dangerous story I can think of. One day we were playing golf at Green Valley and there was a slow fivesome in front of us. I was going to yell at them and my caddy blanched. "No boss, don't even think it!"

She told me one of the slow golfers was a well-known hit man and he had a gun in his bag. I decided slow golf was just fine.

Mike Neun

As for me, I've never, ever had a problem in my 15 years in Thailand. No angry drunks, no fights, I've never seen a fight, no one has bothered me on the street, and I've never experienced road rage here. I feel safe here. I've walked around town at all hours of the night and never had a problem. Lucky for them because I'm from Detroit. I'm sure they'd be impressed.

My Life as a Trained Killer and My Close, Personal Friendship of Clint Eastwood. Trust Me.

L et me preface this by saying Clint Eastwood doesn't have the faintest idea who I am. None. But I did meet him. Let's start with me heading out to basic training.

I walked out the door and looked back. My girlfriend, naked, was waving good bye and laughing. She knew I'd wouldn't see another woman for months and was having a great time rubbing it in. The cab driver was enthused. I was off to join the army. It was 1962, fifty-eight years ago, and I'd been drafted.

At the time I was singing in the Alley Kat Cafe in Seattle and it was not a top of the line nightspot. To get to it you had to walk downstairs from Skid Row at First Avenue and Union Street. It had been a longshoremen's bar when John Timmons bought it. John also owned the Pamir House in the University district, and that was the coffeehouse where I got my start in show business. I think I made seven dollars a night, which doesn't sound like much but I'm sure it's well over ten dollars in today's money. We were folksingers back then, in the transition period between beatniks and hippies and the Pamir House was painted black inside with candles in bottles on the tables.

John bought the Alley Kat with the idea of turning it into a folk bar downtown but it never quite made the transition. Instead it featured a strange mixture of longshoremen and folkies and I learned a great lesson in life. Never, ever mess with longshoremen. Just shut up and try to be friends. In a major blunder, John once thought it would be smart to bring in a bouncer. It was like giving the longshoremen a gift. They had a big argument to see who could take on the bouncer first, and the poor guy didn't last the night.

I was well on my way to Skid Row stardom when I got drafted. I've already told you about my days as a bridge-playing clerk, but that was just the first year. During that year I used to head into Monterey at night and play at the Mission Inn la Cantina in Monterey. I would also sit in with the Dixieland band at the Warehouse on Cannery Row. That band was really, really good. Gary Ryan played banjo and was maybe the best 4-string player I've ever heard. Al Ring played trombone and drums and Dave Tobiason played beautiful rag time and dixieland piano. I played banjo, and I was nowhere near good enough to play with those guys, but we drank a lot and I faked it. I also did some comedy songs.

It was there that I met Don Duncan.

He was sitting at the bar and we had a couple of beers and talked. I didn't think much of it, another army guy from Fort Ord who seemed nice enough. The next day I got back from lunch and the guys in the office asked me if I was in trouble. I didn't think so, but they told me a Special Forces sergeant covered with medals was in looking for me. It turned out that Don was an actual real-life soldier with a bronze star and a hell of a life story. He'd briefed Defense Secretary McNamara in Viet Nam and had done all the stuff the real Special Forces guys did in jungle warfare.

Mike Neun

We became friends and rented a house in Pacific Grove. I commuted to the army.

In time I introduced him to all my hippie musician friends and they had long, serious talks about the war. Don had gone to Vietnam, fought, and then come back to be a recruiter for Special Forces. He'd turned down a bunch of wacko G.I. Joe wannabes. Then he went back for another tour of duty and the guys he'd turned down started showing up in Special Forces. The standards were dropping and the war had changed. No longer were they trying to win the hearts and minds of the Vietnamese, and Don could see the writing on the wall.

He came back and next thing I knew he was on the cover of Ramparts Magazine, in full dress uniform, under the headline, "I Quit." He then wrote a book about Vietnam and the war, which was riveting. I've tried to find it now but I can't. I remember one great passage, where he was sneaking down a jungle trail and looked up to see a tiger right in front of him. He said his rectal pucker factor went up 100%.

He joined the anti-war movement and toured with Joan Baez to speak at rallies. I checked awhile ago and he passed away somewhere in the Midwest, pretty much unknown to the people in the area.

Another time I was in the Warehouse, drinking at the bar, and started talking to an Irishman named Jim Horrigan. We got around to golf and I told him I'd worked at a golf course while I was in high school, cleaning clubs, picking up range balls and running the pro shop. It turned out Jim was the sergeant who ran the Fort Ord golf course. Two days later he had me transferred out there to help run the pro shop and do the books. The first month I did the books I was missing $10,000. Jim was not impressed. He gave me a short course in bookkeeping and we found the $10,000.

Jim was officially the pro, and we had some very good golfers as assistant pros. Rafe Botts was a tall Black guy who could really play. John and Ron Lott were brothers who both got on the tour but didn't last long. Larry O'Leary was another fine golfer from San Francisco, and I'm forgetting the name of the guy who became the head pro at Round Hills Country Club up by San Jose. He was a great guy and great golfer and I hate it that I can't remember his name.

I'd been under the delusion that I was a pretty good golfer, but once I met those guys I realized I wasn't in the same universe. They could all break par and I broke 80 about twice a year. And they all tried for the PGA tour and didn't make it, so it was pretty humbling.

On the other hand, we had great times at the golf course, drinking beer after work, playing the tee game to see who paid. I can't even remember what the tee game is now, but I remember laughing a lot. In the evening we had to take the golf carts down to the barn so we'd each jump in one and play nine holes. You haven't played golf until you've raced 15 other carts down a hole, hitting shots whenever you got to your ball. Fun.

We also got to play all the great courses in the area—Pebble Beach, Cyprus Point, Monterey Peninsula and all the others. I was also singing in town and carousing with my friends so my army experience was quite a ride. So much so, that I almost missed my discharge day. No one told me that you get out one day before the date you came in. People were searching all over the base trying to find me so I could get discharged. I, of course, was playing golf.

This was also about the time I met Clint Eastwood.

One night when I was singing at the Mission Inn la Cantina, someone asked me if I wanted to play golf with Clint Eastwood. At the time, he wasn't the megastar he is today. He was a local, starring in the TV series, Rawhide. Well, that was a pretty big deal and I was excited.

The day before the game, the bartender at the Cantina asked me if I'd ever lifted weights and I said no. He took me to his place and we spent some time in his garage lifting weights. No big deal, right?

The next day I got up to play golf with Clint Eastwood and two other guys at Pebble Beach and I realized I couldn't lift my arms above my waist. Seriously. I got to the course and we played. I tried everything to loosen up, but I could only take a half swing and the ball was flying into parking lots, the ocean, and the yards of the mansions bordering the course. I had a stunningly horrible day, was totally embarrassed, and for some reason Clint never asked me to play with him again.

Much later in life I was opening for Johnny Mathis in Las Vegas and they had a high roller night, when they invited all the mega gamblers to the show. Johnny warned me it would be a lousy audience because high stakes gamblers could care less about shows, they just wanted to get back to the tables.

Clint Eastwood was in that audience and I wanted to do really well, show him what he missed by brushing off that lousy golfer at Pebble Beach. Johnny was right. The audience pretty much ignored the show, I sucked, and Clint Eastwood still has no clue who I am.

I would like to meet him one more time just to tell him how much I love his movie, El Camino. It's an all-time favorite.

ANOTHER DAY IN THE LIFE, WITH SIDE TRIPS

Jintana and I woke up early, around 5 a.m., and lay in bed holding each other for awhile. I'm convinced human bodies are poorly constructed. When you're in bed cuddling with your wife, what do you do with the bottom arm? There's just no place for it. So much for Intelligent Design.

We held each other and drifted in and out of sleep. Then we got up and put water in the hot water pot. It has a magnetic plug and you have to jiggle it until the light goes on. We have a water guy who comes by in a pickup truck filled with cases of bottled water that is really cheap. It costs about 35 baht per case and a case holds 20 bottles of almost a liter each, 35 baht is just over a dollar. I'm going to my calculator now, and it comes to about 5 cents per bottle. I love Thailand. It's not Perrier, but it's safe and they deliver. Speaking of bottled water, did you know that Evian is "naive" spelled backwards?

We pour a 5-cent bottle of water into the hot pot and wash up.

This morning I had half a piece of ciabatta bread left over so I toasted it and ate it with chunky peanut butter.

Jintana's mom is not healthy so this morning I drove her and her mom to Suan Dok Hospital to see three doctors. I dropped them off and went to the Bagel House for breakfast.

Oddly enough, there are three ex-Seattle comedians living in Chiangmai and I messaged one of them, Randy Thompson, to see if he wanted breakfast. Randy is, to put it mildly, unsettled. He moved here a couple of years ago from Hawaii but since then he has been to Spain, Malaysia, a bunch of U.S. cities and a couple other countries I've forgotten. He's moved to Spain twice, for good each time, and now he's back in Chiangmai. Once he moved to Spain to live happily ever after with a woman and it turned into a remake of Steven King's "Misery."

At one point he attempted to make a feature film here in Chiangmai and got the other ex-comedian, Todd Sawyer, to write a script for it. I read the script and it was quite good. Randy got some top-of-the-line equipment and local actors and began filming but the sound never came out right and soon the idea was abandoned. Anyway, he's back now but he didn't answer my message so I ate alone. The Bagel House has great bagels and food of all kinds but I'd eaten a lot of bread lately so I went with muesli and Latte and watched a couple of YouTube XFL football highlights on my cell phone. The Seattle Dragons won, which was good because their helmets were nicer.

Then I drove to Stardome golf course and driving range. I only played the course once and lost a lot of balls in the water but I go to the range a lot. When I got there is was packed but I found a place down near the end and bought two trays of balls. I tipped the guy who brought them because I know those guys make very little money.

A quick word on tipping in Thailand. Thai people tip very little or not at all and it's a cultural thing. This is true also in Australia and some other countries. On the other hand, I spent my American life in the service industry and had a wife who was a waitress before she became a teacher. So I've spent 60 years around people who lived on tips. I literally

Mike Neun

cannot stiff a waiter or service person. My brain would melt. Also, I know most people in Thailand make very little money and compared to them I am rich. So I try to even things out a tiny bit by treating them with respect and tipping. I've had people get angry because I tip too much. Jintana thinks I tip too much. I know I tip too much. But I'm a crazy foreigner and they'll just have to deal with it. The driving range guy does not complain. He does not throw the money back and say, "I don't want this!" I am single-handedly overcoming wealth inequality.

Every day I have something new I want to practice. Today it was finishing the swing because I heard Rory McIlroy say his coach worked on that a lot. It's hard to have a bad swing with a good finish. I think he and Ricky Fowler finish best. They stick the landing, as we say in gymnastics. I've never, ever been around a gymnast.

I practiced slow motion swings, trying to stick the finish. It's hard! I was ending with my left foot spinning out so I worked on that. I'd hit a few balls, then sit down and read stuff on my phone. Mostly sports. The news is too disheartening. After the first tray my back was really hurting, so I lay down on the mat, flat on my back, and read some more sports. People looked at me strangely. Apparently other people don't lie down on driving range mats. Sure enough, when I got up my back was okay and I hit the rest of the balls. The swing felt better but my accuracy was pretty bad.

There's a Swedish pro here named Ken Nillson and he's on a big kick of playing golf rather than playing golf swing. He thinks most people are wasting time on the range trying to develop a pretty swing when they should be on the course learning to score. I'm sure he's got a point, but then I think of range rats like Ben Hogan and Lee Travino and go back to hitting balls. I think the biggest difference between pros and amateurs is the fact that the pros make better contact with the ball. Amateurs are hitting it fat or thin and there's no way you can be consistent doing that.

I love hitting balls.

I like playing golf too, but it's expensive and you have to socialize. For a loner like me, the range is a perfect place to be. I know, it's laughable. An 80-year-old trying to get better at golf. But it beats sitting in bars.

I spent awhile at the range and Jintana and her mom still weren't done so I drove over to get coffee. In the car I listened to a Jeffery Deaver mystery, *Garden of Beasts*. It takes place in Nazi Germany and again I'm amazed how an intelligent country can slip into fascism. I listen to books because music doesn't appeal to me anymore. Maybe I was around it too much.

I drove back to the hospital and picked up Jintana and her mom and then we stopped for lunch at a Thai restaurant on the Canal Road. They had a couple of dishes that would've set my tongue on fire, and I had prawn fried rice and some fried pork with a really good sauce. Jintana and her mom talked while I read more sports news on my iPhone.

We got home and I parked down the street because workmen dug a six-foot deep ditch in front of our house and we couldn't get in the driveway. I assume it's a new sewer. We walked to the house, opened the electric gate, and went inside. I went upstairs to our room, put a yoga mat and pillow on the floor, and lay down on my back again. The driving had made it sore. I fell asleep.

I woke up later and did some writing about army life while Jintana did her ironing. I also got a nice surprise when my brother emailed me about a $600 royalty check I'd gotten for "The Haircut Song." The checks go to Tim's address in Oregon and he deposits them for me. "The Haircut Song?" Well, when I was playing bars all over the northwest one of my major hassles was getting haircuts in strange towns. If you

Mike Neun

were a semi-hippie folksinger trying to get your hair trimmed in Cheyenne, Wyoming, it's a challenge. This was back in the sixties and seventies and long hair was not popular with barbers in those cowboy towns. They wanted to chop it all off. I dealt with it for years and finally thought the hell with it, I'll write a song. It's about a poor bastard getting a haircut in Butte, Montana, then in San Francisco, and then in L.A. It was filled with jokes about redneck barbers, gay barbers and punk rock barbers and I used it as a closer in my shows.

My manager, John Powell, had partnered up with Don Williams, who was Andy Williams' brother. Don managed Ray Stevens, the country singer I mentioned before. He had comic hits like "The Streak" and "Ahab the Arab." They got Ray to record my haircut song and the royalties have been a great addition to my bankroll. He recorded a couple other songs I wrote, including one I really liked called "The Lady on the Radio." It's about a guy driving, listening to the radio, and all of a sudden he hears his wife on a call-in show complaining about their marriage and how lousy he is in bed. Paul Simon never wrote a song like that! I got royalties from it too, but I think the last check was for 11 cents. The "Haircut Song" has been the gift that keeps on giving.

Back to our day.

After a lazy afternoon, Jintana, Awee and I drove over to North Hill Golf Course to sit on the terrace and have dinner. Jintana had her favorite drink, a mojito. She is truly a lightweight when it comes to drinking, as she gets drunk and sleepy on half of a drink. I had pesto pasta with prawns (it was a big prawn day for me) and Awee had a spinach and cheese dish. Jintana wasn't hungry and had a few bites of our food.

Now we're home and she's watching Deadpool on Netflix because I told her it was fun. I'm done with this, so I'll watch something too. I've come to love our quiet nights.

I'M A GUY, LET'S TALK CARS

I know. Guys love things, women love people. So I'll try to include both in this chapter.

When I was a little kid I would hide out in my bedroom and make model cars. None of you will remember this, but back in the Dark Ages we made model cars out of balsa wood. They weren't these plastic things you snap together and say, "Wow, I made a model car!"

No, we had to cut them with Exacto knives and sand them and shape them and I loved that process. I think I also loved sniffing the glue and the paint, which was called dope. Ah yes, a childhood of sniffing glue and dope. I remember making an MG TD and a Jaguar XKE, both of which I think are among the most beautiful cars ever. I also read car magazines—Motor Trend, Hot Rod, Road and Track—and dreamed of the day when I'd get my license and ride around town in a hot car. The girls would be all over me. Sadly, reality is a bitch.

I learned to drive in my mom's '49 DeSoto fluid drive 6, which was quite possibly the slowest car Detroit ever built. It was a sedan, and kind of brown, and the exact opposite of a chick magnet, which everyone knew was a '57 Chevy. We also had a '48 Cadillac, and I think people thought we were richer than we actually were. My dad was smart when it came to money, and he realized that for the price of a new Ford he could buy a two-year-old Cadillac and get a much better car. I didn't get to drive the Cadillac, except for the senior prom, which was a really big deal. My other big achievement was dating a girl whose dad had a Thunderbird and he let me drive it. Whoa. Excitement.

But mostly I drove the DeSoto and I made jokes about it so people would laugh with me instead of at me. Zero to sixty in five minutes, I would boast, and I wasn't far off. Also, it was my mom's car and she made sure I knew it. It wasn't mine. But, and this is a big but, those big bench seats were perfect for making out at the drive-in movies. I wish I could say I was a sex machine in high school, but all we did was kiss a lot. I never got to touch a breast, except in my dreams which were pretty much all the time.

I must've had a car in college because I drove to work at Pizza Pete's and other places, but I can't remember what it was. I have a vivid image of my first ride in a VW Beetle though, and I couldn't believe how small it was. Basically a motorized roller skate that could fit into small spaces. I grew up in Detroit, so I knew it was just an oddity and would never last. I'm right on top of these trends.

The first time I touched a breast was in a car, with a girl who was a college fraternity queen, and I assumed my life had peaked. I don't remember the car, but I sure remember the breast.

But now we come to the good part.

My dad was adventurous and he bought a bright red Austin-Healey 100-6. He drove it for awhile and then bought a Porsche 911, also red. I was in the army at the time and my dad asked if I wanted the Healey. Was he kidding? Of course I did and we worked out a payment plan. I don't remember how I got it down to Fort Ord, but I was the only private there

Mike Neun

with a bright red sports car who was stationed at the golf course and sang in a bar in Monterey. I was not living under the radar.

Maybe there was some resentment. At Fort Ord, when we were clerks, we all issued ourselves two passes. One stayed at headquarters and we carried the other one with us at all times. This eliminated the need to sign in and out, and we thought we were pretty clever. I did too, until one day I drove onto the base, showed my pass to the guard at the gate, and he said, "We're going to check to make sure you signed out."

Busted.

I figured I was AWOL and looking at time in the stockade. I sat there for at least 15 minutes before he came out and said, "Okay, you're good to go."

I almost said, "What?" But I kept my mouth shut and drove on. A couple days later a clerk friend said, "Did we give you a little scare?"

It turned out he was on duty when the guard called and he figured out what was going on. He knew I hadn't signed out and would be sweating bullets, so he told the guard to hang on while he checked the roster. Then he smoked a leisurely cigarette and came back to say, yeah, I'd signed out. The bastard! All the clerks thought it was quite funny.

I loved the Healy. I loved to take it on the twisty roads around Monterey and play race car driver. After I got out of the army I stayed in Monterey and kept playing at the Mission In la Cantina. I also did odd gigs around town, including the grand opening of Becky's Burger Pit (on a flatbed truck with the band from the Warehouse). Obviously I was just inches from the big time.

One time I was speeding down one of the roads, top down, squealing through the curves, and a cop pulled me over. Damn. He came up and said, "Going a little fast weren't you?" I admitted I was. Then he took a closer look at me.

"Hey, aren't you the guy who played the FBI convention in Carmel?" I said I was, and he said he enjoyed the show and let me off with a warning. My first perk.

Another time, after a hard night of partying I was driving a guy home. I didn't know him well, but I'd figured out he was kind of a loudmouth know-it-all drunk. I just wanted to get him out of the car, so I was going too fast. A cop pulled us over, and the guy said, "Let me handle this, I'll talk our way out." I told him to shut the fuck up. The policeman walked up to the car and said, "You guys been doing a little drinking?"

I said, "We've been doing a lot. We're drunk, and I'm guilty."

He stared at me and laughed. "Well, I've never heard that before."

This was before the days of cracking down on drunk drivers and he said as long as it was 4 a.m. and the streets were empty he'd let me go but he was going to follow me to make sure I drove very slowly. I sobered up in about 15 seconds and drove home. Very slowly.

In Monterey I got to know a guy named Jack (again, names aren't my strong point) who owned the foreign car dealership. We played golf together a couple of times. One day I took my Healey in for a repair and he gave me a loaner to drive. A Bentley. Yes, a Bentley! I called up my friends and we drove that thing for hours, pretending we were rich.

The Austin-Healey had the most beautiful sound of any car I ever owned. A couple years later I was working with Brian Bressler and Ron Long at Turk's Straw Hat in Portland, Oregon. Afterwards I would drive home about 3 a.m. through the city with that exhaust sound echoing off the buildings. Beautiful.

There was no stage at Turk's so we would set up on the ledge behind the bar and sing. The place was loud and lots of times people couldn't even hear us so we'd just sing any words

Mike Neun

that came to mind. Sometimes we'd just sing swear words. I have no idea how we kept that job because we were pretty primitive. We didn't even know the names of chords. D was the Triangle, C was the one we started on, and F was "the hard one." We'd just wing it and Brian and Ron would do physical comedy and I'd do comedy songs. Ron was a good singer and played bass. We all drank a lot. One night, as we were singing, Ron leaned over to me and whispered, "What song are we playing?"

Brian used to tell a joke on stage about great white hunters and a gorilla, and a reporter wrote that we sang and told shaggy gorilla stories. Later, someone asked us what the name of the group was and Brian blurted out, "The Shaggy Gorillas Minus One Buffalo Fish." The band, under that name, with different people coming in and out, lasted 8 or 10 years.

We got booked to play in Seattle during the world's fair. We were going to play on an old cruise ship that was being used as a hotel and it was a nice gig for us. We stayed with some friends in a house next to the Tri Delt sorority house at the University of Washington and the night before we were scheduled to start we had a huge party. In our act we used to do a slow motion fight, so at the party Brian decided it would be great to have a slow motion riot—a giant slow motion fight with everyone involved. It was great, and people were falling slow motion over tables and chairs and getting hit with slow motion lamps and beer bottles. It was a huge success. The next night it was time to go play our opening night and we couldn't find Ron. We searched, but came up empty, so Brian and I went to play the gig and immediately got fired. Apparently when they hired a trio they wanted three people to show up. How picky is that?

It turned out that during the slow motion fight, Ron had fallen, slow motion, down the stairs to the basement. He thought the fall was a work of art, but then he passed out, and stayed passed out all the next day and well into the evening. No one had thought to look down there.

Ron's story was very sad. He was a fine bass player, a good singer, and an artist. Great guy. But he got hooked on amphetamines and the last time I saw him he couldn't construct a complete sentence. He died very young.

Remember Turk's Straw Hat? Across the street there was another night club where they had strippers. Or go-go dancers, I can't remember. But a comedian named Pete Barbutti was playing there and that's when we first met Pete. He later became a mainstay at Harold's Casino in Reno and he also appeared on the Tonight Show about 30 times. Johnny Carson loved him, and so did the band. Pete was a jazz musician who did really hip comedy and in a lounge, with a couple musicians backing him, he was astoundingly funny. Just fucking brilliant.

We became friends and our paths kept crossing over the years. One day he called me and asked if I wanted to do a roast. I said sure, who are we roasting? He said, "Chuck Yeager." Yeager was the test pilot who flew the experimental plane outside the atmosphere and was really famous at the time. I told Pete I didn't know a thing about the guy so Pete sent me his biography. I read the book and Pete called about a week before the show. "What'd you think?" he asked.

I told him I really didn't like the guy. He laughed and agreed with me. We did the roast in Las Vegas and it went well.

One time I caught a show Pete was doing in Sacramento and he had an interpreter for the deaf working with him. Pete could stretch a joke forever, and he did one about a covered wagon in the desert. I have no idea what the joke was, but the interplay between him and the deaf interpreter was one of the funniest things I've ever seen. A masterpiece.

Mike Neun

Oh right. I was talking about cars. I can't remember how it happened but after the red Austin-Healey 100-6 I graduated to a white Austin-Healey 3000. I loved those cars but they were absolutely the worst road cars ever. If something went wrong you were doomed. Try to find an Austin-Healey mechanic in Boise, Idaho, or Helena, Montana. I got pretty good at the easy stuff—setting the points and changing plugs and replacing hoses. I could also tune the two SU carburetors by the sound they made. But that was about it.

One night I was driving over the pass between Oregon and California in the middle of a snowstorm and all the lights went out. No headlights, so I couldn't see a damn thing, and no taillights or brake lights, so if I slowed down no one was going to see me. A small, white car in a snow storm? Not a chance. I pulled over to the shoulder and drove through the storm, expecting any minute to be run over by an 18-wheeler. Ah, sports cars, always exciting.

The worst was in another blizzard when Brian and I were driving from Portland to Sun Valley. Before we set off we walked out to the car and found we had a flat tire. We figured we'd drive that afternoon and get it fixed when we stopped for the night. We set out and a blizzard hit us just outside of Pendleton, Oregon. Wind was blowing, the snow was coming down hard, and we were sliding all over the highway. We decided to put on the chains and that was a treat. Putting on chains in the dark in the middle of a blizzard was definitely not fun. Then we plunged on through the storm and bam, we got a flat tire. With a flat spare tire in the trunk. It was one of the rear tires so we had to take that chain off. More fun, jacking up a car in a blizzard, taking off a frozen, iced-up tire chain. Now we were driving on a flat tire and one with a chain, on the shoulder, doing about 10 miles an hour, trying to make it to the grand metropolis of Lime, Oregon.

We went a few miles and bam, the other rear tire went flat. Again, we jacked up the car and took off a frozen, iced-up chain. Fun. Now we were driving on two flat tires, weaving down the side of the highway, and finally we made it to Lime. It was late at night, everything closed, but we managed to wake up a motel manager and get a couple of rooms. The hot showers were blissful and so were the beds.

The next day people stared as we drove through the center of town on two flat tires and found a tire shop. The guy put the Healey up on a hoist and took off the wheels. He took a look at the tires and said, "Where the hell did you get these chains put on?"

We knew something was up and that telling the truth was definitely not an option. We mumbled something about a garage back towards Portland and he exclaimed, "Well, the idiots put the chains on inside out and the cleats ate through the tires! If I were you I'd head back there and raise hell!"

We assured him that we'd do just that and swore a bit about those dumb bastards who put on the chains. Luckily, he had a couple of tires that fit and put them on. Then he patched the spare and we drove out of town bitching about those dumb bastards who put on the chains at that mythical garage.

The white Austin Healey suffered a sad death and again snow was involved. I was driving to Aspen, Colorado, to play at the Red Onion. It was the middle of winter and the highway was snow packed. I was driving alone, making pretty good time, when I saw a clump of snow on the road. I knew if I swerved to go around I could lose control and go off the road, so I straddled it. Well, it wasn't a clump of snow. It was a snow-covered rock and it took out the entire bottom of the engine and transmission. Damn.

A guy gave me a ride into a nearby town and I got someone to go tow the Healey to a garage, and later back to Portland. But I couldn't afford to fix it so it languished in my parents' car port. I guess it languished too long because without bothering to tell me they got rid of it. If you didn't take care of cocker spaniels or Austin-Healeys at our house you'd come home and find them gone.

Meanwhile, back in Colorado, I had to get to the Aspen gig so I asked if I could pay someone to drive me there. A guy at the garage said he would and we jumped into his car. I knew we were in trouble. It was a muscle car with huge rear tires and we spent five hours sliding all over the snow-covered mountain highway, at one point stopping just inches short of a cliff. Scary.

My next car was a Plymouth Barracuda and it was a great ski car. The back seat folded down and you could throw in lots of skis. I also got the small V-8 engine because I'd learned my lesson about overpowered cars in snow country. No muscle cars for me.

So I had a good car and one night Brian and I auditioned at the Purple Onion in San Francisco. We failed and dealt with it in the traditional musician's fashion—we got roaring drunk. We were staggering down some street in North Beach and a little Black kid came up and said, "Hey mister, want to buy a raffle ticket?"

Brian said, "I don't, but my friend's drunk and he'll buy it." I said sure, I'll buy the ticket and gave him a couple bucks. It was a raffle for Synanon, the drug rehab place in San Francisco, and we promptly forgot all about it.

Three or four months later we were playing the Royal Lanai, a bar in Waikiki, Hawaii, and I got a call from the mainland. I had won the raffle! The prize was a Ford Mustang. We had two months to go on our Hawaii gig and I'd just bought the Barracuda so I realized I didn't need another car. I had a Monterey friend go collect the car, sell it and send me the money. Brian was really pissed.

One final blizzard story. I drove the Barracuda back to Ketchum, Idaho, from an opening act gig in Lake Tahoe and again it was snowing. I drove straight through, about 12 hours, with stops for meals and coffee and I finally made it to Ketchum. I remember singing with joy. I was home!

I drove through town, turned down to our cabin, and went to turn right at the T-junction 50 yards from home. Wrong. The road had iced up and instead of turning I went straight ahead into a big snow drift, right up to the windshield. 50 yards from home! And I couldn't leave it there because the next car would hit the ice and crash into mine. Dead tired, swearing, I spent two hours digging out the car and putting on chains so I could get enough grip to get the car out of the drift.

I live in Chiangmai now. No snow. No winter. I am a happy camper.

Mike Neun

COMEDIAN ON ICE

Remember the ice show and the gay skaters in Ketchum? Here's the whole story of those shows.

One day my manager called and asked if I wanted to be in an ice show with Peggy Fleming, the Olympic gold medalist. What the hell would I do in an ice show? The answer was simple, I'd walk out on the ice in a pair of golf shoes (spikes so I wouldn't slip) and do 15 or 20 minutes between numbers while the skaters changed costumes.

The show was produced by Bob Banner, who was a highly respected Hollywood producer, and directed by Dick (whose last name I've forgotten), a former Mousketeer on the Mickey Mouse Club TV show. We had four variety acts in the show. Me, Walt Wagner, who was a pianist who always got a standing ovation when he played MacArthur Park, a sister singing group of four Black girls, and a skating comedy act. I, of course, fell in love with one of the girl singers and she did not fall in love with me. Girls can be so blind...

In our first rehearsal Dick showed us our costumes for the finale and we all refused. They were like Up With People costumes, with sequined red white and blue outfits and spangled straw hats. Remember, this was the early '70s and we were still part of the hippie culture. Not a chance in hell we were going to wear those costumes. Dick backed down and we got to wear what we wanted.

This brings back a memory of two friends of mine, Dennis Coats and Gary Carlson. They were wonderful musicians and singers, with Dennis on 5-string banjo and Gary on guitar. They were dope-smoking, tequila-drinking bluegrass guys. Dennis was also a pool shark and played big money games.

One night a guy came up and said he could get them a high-paying gig at Disneyland and they got excited. They flew down to L.A., passed the audition with flying colors, and the director said, "You're hired."

Okay! It was a big step up from playing loud bars in the Northwest. Then the director said, "Now we have to get you fitted for costumes."

Dennis said, "We don't need costumes, we just play in jeans and shirts."

The director said, "No, you have to wear bear costumes."

So much for Disneyland.

Here's the deal on the ice show. It was called "Concert on Ice" and the plan was to play a series of theaters-in-the-round up the east coast and then do the show at Christmas at Harrah's in Lake Tahoe. The theaters held between 2500 to 3500 people and the show would be done on a portable ice rink that would cover the stage. It was much smaller than the hockey rinks they used for Ice Capades, but it was amazing what the skaters could do. With Peggy were a pairs team of Willie Bietak and Cathy Steele, and eight chorus line skaters—four boys and four girls.

I did that show for (I think) three years. No wait, it must've been four. Peggy did it two years, then Scott Hamilton came in and starred, and then Dorothy Hammil.

I had never worked a theater in the round before, and I certainly had never walked out on a patch of ice to do

Mike Neun

comedy. Also, I'd never walked out on a wet patch of ice in metal spikes carrying a piece of electric equipment. I could see the headlines, "Comedian Killed by Microphones!"

Later we realized the ice was cut up by then so I didn't need spikes. The sound guys assured me there was no electrical danger but I immediately switched to rubber-soled shoes.

I followed a skating number with Peggy done to the song, *Song Sung Blue*, and I can't tell you how sick I got of that song. Just thinking about it now makes me cringe. Peggy, on the other hand, was the ultimate class act. She was quiet and gracious and a great skater. Her mom was a skater's mom, kind of overbearing, but we found she could loosen up too. Remember streaking? Back then it was great fun to run naked through a football game or a convention and one night at Harrah's Peggy's mom convinced our bass player to streak my show. He ran across the ice in white boots and nothing else and it brought the house down. I learned a valuable lesson that night. If you get streaked, that will be the highlight of the show and if you have five minutes to go you're doomed. My big closer was kind of anticlimactic.

I'd never been around gay guys much, but the boy skaters in the show changed that. They were extremely gay and their humor just blew me away. The girl skaters were beautiful, and of course I fell in love with them. Again, nothing. Apparently being the big-time, guitar-playing comedy star was not the chick magnet I'd expected it to be.

Willie and Cathy, the pairs team, were also Olympic medalists and very classy people. They were also the ones who taught me how tough skaters were. I'd never thought about that before, but falling on ice is like falling on concrete. So when you see those blooper reels of skaters falling, you're watching a painful experience. Willie and Cathy did a move where he'd hold her by one ankle and spin her around with her head very close to the ice. It was impressive. But one night her skate was wet and his grip slipped. Cathy flew out of his grasp and slid across the ice into the orchestra pit. The musicians caught her, but she was pretty scraped up. She got back on the ice and finished the act with blood running down a scrape on her leg. The next night she was back, with heavy makeup on the wound, doing the same move with Willie. Tough, these skaters.

Later on we had Tai Babilonia and Randy Gardner do the pairs routine. They came out of two upright tubes that would fill with smoke and then they would appear. One night something went wrong with the smoke machine and Tai got burned by hot oil, but the next night they were back out there, doing the show. As I say, tough.

A smart person would've bought a pair of skates and learned from the experts. For some reason that never occurred to me. Instead, I bought a sewing machine. I have no idea why, but the days were long and we were products of the Sixties and loved to experiment with clothes. It was still the era of tie-dyes and bell bottoms and flowers in the hair. So I made shirts that I thought were pretty impressive but when I think of them now I get embarrassed. Maybe that's what put off the girl skaters.

Ah! Another memory. The show carried four musicians—a piano player/conductor, bass, drums and guitar. When we got to a city, they'd fill out the band with local concert musicians and one of them had to be a French horn player because there was a specific part for him in Song Sung Blue. Apparently it was a difficult part because every night we'd stand off stage and wait to see if the French horn would hit the high note. I think we wagered on it and it was a 50-50 bet. The solo would climb and climb to that high note and...

Besides doing my comedy I'd do a number with one of the skaters where I'd sing "Mister Bojangles" and he would

134   Mike Neun

skate to it. Actually, I would kind of talk and sing, like a story. It was a nice number, but one night Dick the director thought he could do the skating part better. He'd been a dancer and I'm sure he had chops, but when he did it the audience thought it was a comedy number and it didn't go well. I felt sorry for him.

Ice skating comics:

In those four years we had two skating comedy acts. Both were old-time professionals with about ten minutes of killer material that they lived on for years. The first was Eric Waite, and there'd be a big production number with a prince and princess surrounded by girl skaters in tutus carrying u-shaped flowered hoops. One of those girl skaters would be Eric, and he would lose control of one end of the hoop and start chasing it around. From there it would go into classic slapstick and the audiences loved it.

The other act replaced Eric after the first two years. I wish I could remember their names but they were introduced as ice dancing champions. They were husband and wife and would come out elegantly in tuxedo and ball gown, skating beautifully. Then a metal light shade would fall from the ceiling, he would trip on it and do a tremendous fall. The audience would gasp. He'd get up, bravely, and start skating again. The audience would applaud madly. What courage, what a professional! But then more things would go wrong. His stiff collar would fly loose, his pants would fall, and again it was a beautiful piece of slapstick comedy. Money in the bank.

They were great years and I got to know a whole new subculture. I also found out that there's an art to making ice. Too warm and it gets slushy and slow to skate on. Too cold and it's like cement and the grooves can trip up skaters. So we had two ice technicians and their job was to find that perfect temperature as the temperature and humidity in the theaters fluctuated. Not easy.

Also I worked with one of my oldest friends, Walt Wagner. Walt is a really gifted Seattle pianist who studied classical music and then drifted into jazz and pop. He is kind of the golden boy of music, able to light up a room with his smile and bring an audience to their feet with his music. I, of course, hated that. Goddam audiences. Every night in the show he'd play MacArthur Park, build to a giant climax, and get a standing ovation. Every night I'd do my show and get a fine ovation from a bunch of people glued to their seats. Walt was flamboyant, I was understated. MacArthur Park was a stupid song. Okay, I was a little bitter but I concealed it well.

During the second tour of the show, some of us decided it would be fun to camp out instead of staying in motels. We'd either find a KOA or camp out behind the theater. The funny part was that Walt drove a Lincoln Towncar, which was huge, even in those days of Detroit monsters. We couldn't wait so see him drive up to a KOA camping space in his luxury limo, get out and pitch a pup tent.

Walt and I both had John Powell as a manager so we played a lot of shows together over the years. He was hugely popular in the Northwest and would fill up nightclubs wherever he played. The only time he failed baffled him until I explained what went wrong. John booked him on a Seabourn cruise ship, which would've given him a nice job option if he'd succeeded. As usual, he got standing ovations, and was kind of stunned when he didn't get booked again. I knew what had happened because I'd played that line a lot. The cruise director on that ship also played piano and did occasional shows, and he was no match for Walt. I'm sure he gave him a bad review. The world isn't fair, and those ships lost a really good performer.

So there you have it. Every now and then I still have a nightmare where I walk out on a piece of ice with a microphone stand, set it down, and get electrocuted. I bet I would've gotten a standing ovation.

P.S. It took me three weeks, but I just remembered Dick's last name. Foster. A mind is a terrible thing to waste.

WHY DO LOUSY ATHLETES LOVE SPORTS?

John R. Tunis wrote sports books and they were always about some skinny kid with glasses who discovered a rare talent and became a big league star. One was about a kid who spent hours hitting a baseball up on a roof and then hitting it up there again when it came down. He could always make contact no matter where the ball came from. He got to the big leagues because he would just foul off pitches until the pitcher finally walked him. His on base percentage was a thousand. As a skinny kid with glasses, I devoured those books and I knew that someday I would discover a secret talent and become one of the greatest sports stars of all time.

As I grew older I realized I couldn't run fast, couldn't jump, and hated physical contact. Other than that, I was a great athlete.

Luckily, my parents had lots of books and I also found Robert Benchley, Dorothy Parker, and other humorous authors I will remember tonight about 4 a.m. Benchley wrote stuff like *The Sex Life of a Newt* which I thought was very funny because I was a young boy and the title had *Sex* in it.

Because of these great authors I tried to inject humor into all the school essays I wrote and in the back of my mind I like to think teachers and professors thanked me for breaking the monotony.

It's a good thing I studied and worked at humor because I wasn't headed for sports stardom. Ah, but I could play ping pong. We had a ping pong table in the basement and one of my fondest memories is playing hours with my dad. We never bothered to keep score and I like to think it was like Black guys playing basketball, where the quality of the shots was much more important than numbers. I loved those nights.

In the dorms at the University of Washington there was a Korean student down the hall and we had great nights playing ping pong on the tables on the ground floor.

I hit the wall on a cruise ship out of Hong Kong. I was working a long contract on the ship, maybe two months, and in the middle of it was a charter with 700 Hong Kong Chinese people. I was useless as a comedian (my Chinese is nonexistent) so I basically had the week off and I played ping pong. I got hammered. Little Chinese grandmothers were beating the hell out of me. Apparently ping pong is a big deal in China.

I played little league baseball and was a complete bust, except for one play. For some reason I was at shortstop and a kid hit a line drive right at me. I put up my glove to protect my face and the ball hit it and stuck. I had made a catch! I don't know who was more stunned, me or the coach.

I know my dad wanted me to help me be an athlete and we played catch on the front lawn. Again, good memories. But he also wanted to toughen me up so we had boxing gloves. All I remember about that is the time he hit me in the nose and I ran crying to my mom. Mike Tyson was safe.

I played center on the junior high football team and that was a good place for me. I could hike the ball and then just

Mike Neun

get buried in the line play, trying to block where no one could see me. You know those football blooper reels where the center gets the count wrong and the whole team is running the play while he holds onto the ball? I did that. I could've sworn the quarterback said hike it on five. Ten other guys knew it was one. All I know is that I was holding the ball and all my teammates were running around swearing.

In my day there was a lot of pressure to be a man, so after painful soul searching I decided to go out for high school football. Ours was a very small high school and if you were a guy and you didn't go out for football, you were pretty much gay. Now? No big deal. Back then? It was a big deal.

Football practice had already started, so I gathered up my courage one evening and pedaled my bike over to the coach's house to ask if I could try out for the team. It was a huge, earth-shaking moment for me, but he seemed kind of surprised I was there and said, "Sure."

I lasted three days. It ended the day we had head-on tackling practice where one guy had the ball and ran at the guy who was supposed to tackle him. Every school has a Jim Fisher. Jim Fisher is the guy who's flunked a couple of grades and works at the gas station. He's big and tough. That's who I drew and he laid me out cold. My football career halted on the spot. No Mas.

I did play basketball and eventually made the varsity team as the sixth man on a really good five-man team. In those days none of us knew that players like Magic Johnson and Larry Bird would shoot 700 jump shots a day. I was just good enough to make the team but not good enough to date a cheerleader.

Years later I was working on cruise ship and Paul McFarland was the cruise director. Paul had played football at the University of Montana and then made it to pre-season with the San Diego Chargers as a linebacker. One day, I have no idea where, we played some one-on-one basketball. I just assumed he was big and loved to hit people but I was wrong. He was amazingly quick and again I realized the difference between my athletic dreams and reality.

On the ships we played paddle tennis and I loved it much more than tennis. The court was smaller and we played with tennis balls with the air let out. You'd just poke a surgical needle in, let the air out and the balls were much less lively. It was a great game, kind of between ping pong and tennis, and Paul and I would play a lot. In ports we played tennis and again, I was mediocre but I felt I wasn't horrible. Then we got to Vietnam.

Paul and I were walking through Saigon and there were some Vietnamese guys playing tennis. They were rank beginners, just paddling the ball softly back and forth and I could literally see the thought balloons above our heads with "We'll show these guys how the game is played."

I should preface this by saying that Paul is 6'4" tall, very strong, and can hit a 100 mph serve. The good news was that it seldom went in. So in our tennis games he would blast balls all over the court and I would spend my time calling "Out."

Well, on this day he had the service games of his life. I spent about 45 minutes waving at aces and it was like PeeWee Herman playing Roger Federer. Embarrassing enough, but afterwards one of the Vietnamese guys came up to me and said, "First time play tennis?"

I love sports.

Mike Neun

GUYS, LET ME HELP YOU WITH RELATIONSHIPS

This will be the shortest chapter in the book.

Rule Number One: Do not listen to anything I have to say about relationships.

I am 80 years old and still clueless. The only reason Jintana and I are still together is that she is really good at relationships and I've calmed down.

Here are my greatest relationship lessons:

Guys, if you're trying to meet girls this is the one method most men never think to use. Be honest. I grew up in the days when guys tried hard to be cool. We tried to figure out cool things to say to women and none of them worked.

The best way to be cool was to be the quarterback on the football team. Then you could say, "Duh", and it would be cool. The other way to be cool was to be an outlaw. Women love bad boys and I will never understand that. Protection? Don't mess with me or my boyfriend will beat you up? Maybe.

But if you're going to talk to women, just tell the truth. For one thing, it will surprise the women and they will be grateful. They won't have to cut through the usual bullshit. If you meet a beautiful woman and are scared and shy, say, "I'm scared and shy."

If you're broke and living with your parents, say you're broke and living with your parents. Don't fake it. If you're in that situation and pretend to be a big-time executive, you better hope you're in a sitcom, because it doesn't work in real life.

The second lesson: If you're in a relationship, learn to shut up. If something is wrong, the male tendency is to try to fix it. Right now! Don't do that. Just shut up. Maybe shut up for a day or two. You'll be amazed how many problems work themselves out if you just let them settle for awhile.

Finally if you're alone, desperate to meet someone, that desperation will drive them away. Being needy is an absolute turn off. How do you solve that? Work on yourself. Learn some skills, educate yourself, get in shape, and try to be a better person. People are attracted to that and it's far better to have them coming to you than you trying to chase them. If that fails, buy a guitar and become a lead singer in a rock band.

That's it. It took me years to learn those things and it's quite possible I'll screw them up tomorrow because hey, I'm a guy.

Mike Neun

THAI DRIVERS ARE CRAZY

Every foreigner who comes here says that and they're all wrong. It's just that there's a different system here, based on an entirely different culture. It works just fine.

First, you have to understand the rules.

One. Thai people drive on the wrong side of the road. It's their way of thinning out the herd of tourists. In Thailand we drive on the left and the steering wheel is on the right side of the car. About once a year I get in the car on the wrong side and think someone has stolen the steering wheel.

Two. Double yellow lines and yellow lines on your side of the median are just suggestions. In America, these lines say, "Do not pass." In Thailand they say, "Maybe you shouldn't pass but if you see an opening, go for it." Thai drivers pass anywhere at any time. You're in the middle of the city with a slow guy in front of you? Give it a shot. On a blind curve or a hill where you can't see oncoming traffic? Maybe you shouldn't pass but what the hell. Drivers in oncoming cars are familiar with this rule and will pull onto the shoulder to give you room. This is wise, because the alternative is a head-on collision.

Three. Every street and highway has more lanes than you think. If traffic is jammed, Thai drivers will create new lanes on the shoulders or in the median. In times of high traffic, every bit of every road is used and people know this. Also, there are thousands of motorbikes and they will create three new lanes on any street.

Four: The normal passing lane is on the right, but if it's easier to pass on the left, no problem.

Five: Tailgating is the national sport. Deal with it.

Six: Cutting in and out of traffic is national sport number two, so you learn to watch the front wheels of the other cars. They could turn at any time.

Seven: Stoplights. Stoplights are different here because if it's a four-way intersection they only allow one way at a time. This means if you hit a light that just turned red, you will have a long wait. Thai people deal with this by assuming a yellow light means only 5 or 10 more cars can go through. If you stop for a yellow light, you will get rear-ended. People don't want to wait for that long red light. To make this doubly exciting, motorbike riders who see their light about to turn green will sneak into the intersection and get hammered by cars running the red. This could be a tiny flaw in the system.

Eight: If you're rich, no rules apply. So it's like most other countries. There are horror stories of rich people in Mercedes plowing into crowds or hammering motorbikes and getting off with a fine.

Nine: In America, if you flash your headlights it means, "Go ahead, I'll give you the right of way." In Thailand it means, "Don't even think of entering the intersection, I'm coming through fast."

Ten: Helmet laws. Thailand has helmet laws for people on motorbikes and motorcycles. Foreigners scream because lots of Thai people don't wear helmets but there are reasons. If you're a really poor person, you might have the

Mike Neun

choice between buying a helmet or feeding your family for a month. I don't know about you, but I'd go for the food. Also, Thailand summers are very hot, so I'm thinking a helmet in intense heat is like putting on a crockpot and feeling your brain boil. Finally, if you're a woman and you've spent a lot of time getting your hair just right, say, for a job interview, would you put on a helmet? It's a complex situation, and the obvious rebuttal to those people who don't wear helmets is death. Good hair or death? Not a great choice.

You also have random police checkpoints where they catch the people without helmets and fine them. There are two reasons for this. Safety, and the fact that the police are paid very little money. It's understood that this is a way to augment their income and a lot of those fines go into pockets. As I said, it's a cultural thing.

Eleven: I have never, ever seen a car on the highway pulled over by the police in Thailand. It must happen, but I've never seen it, so the highways are kind of like the wild west. The only time I've seen cars stopped are random police checks for drunk drivers. Caution. If you are drunk, it's a big deal and you have jail in your future. Unless you're really rich or know the chief of police. Side note: This is not just a Thai thing. I just remembered being on a ship pulling into Acapulco and on a cliff overlooking the harbor were two huge mansions. I asked the local guide who they belonged to. She said one was owned by Sylvester Stallone. The other by the chief of police.

Twelve: There are no driving rules for motorbikes. They will go anywhere at any time and it's your job to dodge them. If it's faster to go the wrong way up a one-way street, a motorbike will do that. I had a friend who was walking and got hit by a motorbike going the wrong way on the sidewalk! If a motorbike wants to pass you on your left, from your blind spot, they will do that. If you're driving a car, it's like playing a video game where motorbikes can attack from any point on the compass and you have to avoid them. I had a friend say he was a much better driver since he came here because he was 100% more alert. He was right.

Thirteen: There are other things to watch out for. Pedicabs, Tuk Tuks (the 3-wheeled taxis), songtaws (the red pickup truck buses), bicycles, Chinese people who walk in the middle of streets, drunks (the town drunk in our village chose to sleep in the middle of our road one night), loudspeaker trucks that go very slow, water buffalo (one guy used to walk his on the road I drove to play golf), chickens, dogs, and lots of strange and wonderful obstacles. Again, be alert.

Fourteen: If you're a pedestrian and you think traffic is going to stop so you can cross, you are going to die. In Thailand, vehicles have the right of way and you have to wait for a gap in traffic and then go for it. But look both ways! Also, Thai people hate foreigners who hold up their hands like, "I'm important, I'm going to cross, and you have to stop." It may work, but it pisses them off. The accepted method is to make eye contact with the driver and give a slight bow, asking permission to cross. If the driver nods, you're good to go. It is much more polite and I vote for that.

Fifteen: You can't blow your horn unless it's an emergency. I love this law. Thai cities are so much quieter than places like New York city or all of China. I once rode a tour bus from Tianjin, China, to the Great Wall and we actually timed the driver. He blew his horn every 45 seconds whether he needed to or not. For three hours! It was insane. Anyway, Thai drivers don't blow their horns. If they do, it's an emergency or you've done something that really, really, pisses them off. If so, wai and apologize. Profusely. Road rage has been known to be lethal here. There are guns in some cars. Pretend you're in Texas.

Sixteen: If there is an accident, you never drive the cars or the motorbikes to the side of the road and let traffic pass. No! You call the police and insurance people so they can come see the exact scene of the crime and take pictures. This could take time, and traffic will back up for miles. You have to just accept it, because that's the way it's done.

Seventeen: Sidewalks. If you are walking on a sidewalk, it is exciting. There will be trees in the middle, broken concrete, ditches, holes, sign poles—all kinds of obstacles and you have to stay alert. I had a friend who broke his hip tripping over an iron bolt sticking up from the sidewalk. Look down, watch where you're going.

Finally, don't drink and drive. Not because of the law, but because it's morally wrong. My worst nightmare would be to be impaired and hit some kid on a motorbike. My life as I know it would be over.

All that being said, I enjoy driving in Thailand. It's far more interesting than driving in the states and far more creative. I've been here 15 years and I keep reminding myself that I am not in a hurry and have not mastered Thai driving. Overconfidence kills. But it's the best video game ever.

RACISM SUCKS.

I know what you're thinking. Who better to talk about racism than an 80-year-old white guy from the suburbs. I'm sure he'll clear it all up. Fat chance.

I grew up in Detroit. Ah, you're thinking, that's where he got his street cred. Nope. Detroit was a thriving city when I was a kid and we lived in a middle-class area. There were people in Detroit from all minority groups, drawn by the lure of jobs in the car companies, but I don't think there were any black or brown people in my grade school.

Then we moved south to Grosse Ile, an island in the Detroit River, and it was all white too. The closest I came to Black people was when a friend took me to a Fats Domino concert. You talk about culture shock! Oh wait, we also played basketball against some Black high schools from River Rouge and Inkster. But I played so little I still had no interaction with Black people. At home, my mom was the liberal and my dad was the conservative. I think he grew up with racism but he was a smart guy and wised up.

College was the first time I ever spent in classrooms and dorms with people of other races and it was fascinating.

In my last year of college I got elected president of my fraternity and the only Black person there was our cook. It was dead wrong. Racist. Later I resigned from the fraternity because of it but it was way too little and way too late.

Our cook had worked years on the railroads, retired, and now was making money cooking for us. His name was Elmo Johnson and I used to sit around the kitchen talking to him. One time he took me to a Black blues bar and I loved it.

After college I entered the army in 1962 and was of course aware of the Civil Rights movement and Martin Luther King. As a card-carrying bleeding heart, I was a fervent supporter of both but it was hard to go to marches with an army haircut. They would've thought I was a narc.

When it came to race, I couldn't have picked a better career. Music is the great leveler, because musicians know immediately if someone can play and it doesn't matter what race they are. Also, we all did songs from the great Black blues musicians and singers.

That being said, I can honestly say I have no idea what Black people went through back then. None of the books and none of the conversations could give me the true, visceral feeling of what it was to be black or brown in America.

Oh wait. In college I met Barbara Yoshida and we went together for awhile. She became a lifelong friend and we're still in touch. She was the first to give me a true picture of racial stereotypes because her family had been put in an internment camp in Idaho during World War II. Remember that war? When we fought the Germans, Italians and Japanese? Well, there were Germans, Italians and Japanese in America at the time but guess who got put into camps!

Barbara's dad was a farmer, very poor, living in Beaumont, Idaho, with his wife, Michi. Barbara did tell me a couple positive stories about the imprisonment of the Japanese. A guy in their town bought all the stuff the

Mike Neun

Japanese had to sell before they left and kept it for them. How cool is that? Also, some of their neighbors would hollow out watermelons and smuggle stuff into the camps for them. So there were some good people in those communities but the internment was terribly wrong.

I think Barbara's older sister was born in the camp.

When they got out, her dad went back to farming but all three kids made it into college and that's where I met Barbara. Her brother, Bruce, is a stockbroker and manages my vast stock portfolio. He must make fifteen or twenty bucks a year in commissions. Barbara married Ed Berthiaume, who became a Boeing executive and they lived for ten years in Singapore. It was there they introduced me to the watch man.

This has nothing to do with race, but it was fun. These were the first days of fake Rolexes and Guccis and all the rest but I'd never seen one. It was like a spy novel. I went to their apartment and Barbara called a cut-out number and hung up. Another number called her back and a few minutes later a guy showed up with a briefcase full of fake watches. Excitement! I bought three or four for about 30 bucks each. 30 bucks for a Rolex! Those were the days when you could tell they were fakes because the second hand jumped instead of rotating smoothly. I gave one of those Rolexes to John Powell, my manager, and he wore it for years. I told him it was a fake, but he loved it anyway.

So Barbara filled me in on racism against the Japanese.

Want a happy ending? Late in life her mom, Michi, went into real estate. Here was this little grandmother who knew everyone in that part of Idaho and she sold a lot of real estate. They went from her dad dragging irrigation pipe to a nice life on the money Michi brought in.

In the army I met some of the guys from the company band. People said you could find the band barracks because of the smell of pot. A couple of those guys, both Black, used to come sit in at the Mission Inn la Cantina when we had our Sunday jam sessions and one of them taught me the song, *Saturday Night Fish Fry* by Louis Jordan.

Later in life I worked a couple years as an opening act with Johnny Mathis, who was probably the classiest guy I ever met in show business. Here he was, the son of domestic workers, a high jumper in college and one of the greatest singers of all time. He was also Black and gay. Talk about a double whammy. But in the time I knew him, we never talked about race, or being gay, so I missed out on a huge opportunity to learn. He was quiet, thoughtful, and treated the people he worked with really well. He had the same musicians and conductor for years. He sold millions of records, and to see him at his best go on YouTube and watch him sing "Pieces of Dreams" on the Tonight Show. Johnny Carson called it the show's greatest singing performance ever. I agree.

Working with him was ideal for an opening act because Johnny would go on first and do three or four songs. Then he'd introduce me and I'd come on to an audience that was already warmed up with a fine introduction by him. Talk about a dream job.

The other great thing about working with him was that he loved golf. You'd be amazed at the courses you could get on if you had a super star calling up for a tee time. We played some of the best courses in the country. The most memorable was the mega private course in Las Vegas, Shadow Creek. There were small brass nameplates on the lockers with names like Michael Jordan, George H. W. Bush, etc. We played there with Steve Wynn, the billionaire who built the course and owned three or four casinos, including the Bellagio and

Mike Neun

Mirage. I was driving a VW Beetle. For some reason I didn't feel Steve and I had a lot in common.

Steve Wynn suffered from macular degeneration and was losing his eyesight, so he had a pro come along and line up his shots for him. I never was good at being around the rich and famous and it was kind of a weird day for me. I remember impressing people on the range, hitting the ball well, and then going out and playing a lousy round. Johnny, as always, was quiet and kind and shot his usual round in the 80's.

Now I'm married to a Thai lady, Jintana, and I love her deeply. She has given me the thirteen best years of my life. We joke about stupid old white people screwing up Thailand and what lousy drivers they are, usually while I'm driving.

So, about race. It's simple. Racism is stupid. It just is. If you're a racist, you're losing out on knowing some of the best people on the planet.

YO HO HO,
ANOTHER LIFE AT SEA

As I said before, a guy came up to me after a show at Harrah's in Lake Tahoe. I can't remember who I was opening for, maybe Neil Sedaka, but this guy asked, "Have you ever worked cruise ships?"

I told him I'd never thought about it, and four weeks later I boarded a Holland America ship. As always, I was clueless and not big on research so I had no idea what to wear or how to do shows on cruise ships. My dressiest outfit was a brown corduroy suit (it might've been the only one ever made) and boat shoes. Hey, it was a boat!

I had three shows to do, so I tried to split up my material so the last show would be the best. Leave them laughing, right? Nope. On ships, your first show has to work if you want anyone to come back for the next one. I remember David DeHaveland was the cruise director and he was a very elegant Englishman. By the time I got to the third show at the end of the cruise, I knew he was not impressed. Then he saw my suit and said something like, "You're going to wear that?"

I had no choice.

He introduced me kind of apologetically and I did my best stuff and killed. When I walked off stage he looked at me with new eyes and I knew I'd saved the job.

I worked the old Holland America ships, the Veendam and Vollendam, and all I remember is the authorities wouldn't let them into Bermuda because they smoked too much and dirtied up the pristine yachts in the harbor. Those ships were sold soon after and new ones came in. But there were major positives to the job. I'd been working a lot of corporate conventions and while the money was excellent I'd come to hate them with a passion. The setups were just awful for me. Usually they were dinners, with people sitting at round tables. This meant that half the room had their backs to me. Also, my needs were simple. I needed two microphones, one for my acoustic guitar and one for vocal, and a spotlight. Not a lot to ask you would think, but I'd guess about 75% of the gigs fell short. Either there was just one microphone (one venue produced a podium with a mic—try playing a guitar in that situation!) or the buyer would point to a bulb in the ceiling and say, we couldn't find a spotlight, won't that work? Also, most hotel sound systems are incredibly bad. Tinny old speakers in the ceiling and lousy mics are death to an act like me because I speak in a normal voice and don't project like Pavarotti.

The worst, though, were conventions with themes. God save me from themes. One had a circus theme and the guy wanted me to do my show from a cage. Seriously. I declined.

So I had to fight through all that before I even got on stage, if they even had a stage.

One night I was waiting in the kitchen (the hotel equivalent of a green room) and a Mexican waiter looked at my guitar and did a double take. "Wow, man, nice guitar."

I thanked him and asked him if he played. He said a little bit, but not a 12-string. I had some time before I went on so I handed it to him and told him to give it a try. He played a flamenco piece brilliantly. Just awesome. Then he handed it back, thanked me and went out to bus tables. I went out to do my three-chord songs and make a lot of money. The world isn't fair.

Next, the show. There were two options. Either the introduction was short and that meant I started my show while people were finishing desert and the waiters were clattering dishes, or the introduction featured one of the company bigwigs making a long speech and putting everyone to sleep.

Apparently I didn't suck because I kept getting convention bookings. I was making good money and struggling mightily. The good news was I was also playing colleges and they had great sound and lights with competent people working them. In college concerts I felt like I'd died and gone to heaven. They were in theaters with an actual stage and the audience in seats that faced the stage! What a concept! I loved doing colleges. I know that now comedians face all kinds of hassles from political groups but back then college audiences were intelligent and open-minded and I loved them.

Anyway, I was playing a lot of one-nighters, some opening act stuff, and I was intensely lonely. I'm terrible at walking into bars and making friends. Even if I played a couple weeks in a casino, by the time I got to know anyone it was time to move on. I was getting weird and the ships saved me because there were people to hang out with. My favorites were the other entertainers from all over the world, the cruise staff, the lecturers (most of whom were wildly intelligent and interesting), and many of the passengers. I was no longer the lonely weird guy flying from one-nighter to one-nighter. I had friends! Not only that, but as I moved from ship to ship, a lot of those same people would appear. It was a community and I loved it.

I worked Holland America briefly before I got hired by Royal Viking Lines and it could be argued that their three ships, *The Sea, The Sky* and *The Star,* were the number one ships of that era.

I had a couple of major advantages over other comedians on those ships. One, I'd worked in bars for years, covering four hours a night. Also, I'd done all those concerts for PBS-TV, so I had lots of material. I could do three or four different shows on a cruise. Most comedy club or show acts had a solid 45 minutes and not much else.

Second, I'd worked in and around country clubs as a teenager and knew the clientele. We were dealing with wealthy older people and I knew the drill.

Better yet, the three ships were stationed in three different parts of the world. One was in Europe, one in Asia, and one in North and South America. As I was successful, I could work any of the ships so I would pick cruises that went to places I'd never been before. It was glorious, and a huge education.

Enough of that, it's time for random ship stories.

After Royal Viking I worked a lot on the Seabourn ships, which were very elegant and quite a bit smaller than normal cruise ships. Every stateroom was a suite and the original *Seabourn Pride* and *Spirit* only held 215 passengers. Because they were small, they bounced around more in rough seas and while I was a pretty good sailor I did get seasick when it got bad. In rough seas, the best place to be on a ship is down low in the middle of the ship. The worst is in the bow, because it's crashing into waves and bouncing a lot. On one ship I would always go to the show room, low and in the middle of the ship, and I would grab bread and crackers from

Mike Neun

the crew mess because they settle your stomach. If I went late at night there would be a Filipino stewardess there too and we would share bread and crackers. We didn't even talk, we just shared our misery.

One time on a Crystal cruise ship we were docked and they set up a basketball hoop on the tarmac next to the ship. The Filipino crew loved basketball and I did too, so we played. It was the one time on a basketball court where I was the tallest person out there and I felt like Kareem. Their strategy was to get the ball and drive to the hoop. There wasn't a lot of passing or outside shooting but they were quite good at driving into the paint. I did a lot of rebounding and trying to block shots and it was a great day.

In Madras, India, Walt Wagner and I were getting ready to go ashore. I can't remember what ship it was, but obviously not Seabourn with the piano-playing cruise director. We were standing on deck and noticed a bunch of really poor-looking guys with pedicabs—three-wheeled bicycles with a seat in the back. We thought why not get a couple of those to take us on a tour of the town? We could give them a day's work and a nice tip and it would be good for everyone. Dream on.

We got off the ship, hired two pedicab drivers who promised to give us a tour. They pedaled us out the gate, his driver turned left, mine turned right and that's the last we saw of each other. Mine took me to a really rough part of town, got to a square filled with tough-looking guys and stopped. He then informed me it would cost twice as much money to get back to the ship. I looked around, decided I was out gunned, and paid up. I found out later that Walt's driver did the same thing. Terrible, right? Not really, because it became another story to tell on stage.

There were lots of hustles. They had an Egyptian variation at the pyramids where guys offered camel rides for five dollars. Not bad, right? It turned out it was five dollars to get on, ten dollars to get off. In Barcelona they warned us guys would spill something on your shirt and then pick your pocket as they apologized and wiped it off. Lots of scams, but I avoided the hustles and loved walking around exotic places.

St. Petersburg, Russia, is one of the great walking cities in the world and one with an amazing history. We first went there before the Iron Curtain fell, when Russia was very grim and communist and part of every tour was a small, elegant department store in the middle of town. The Russians called it "The Museum" because no normal Russian could afford anything there. For them it was look, but don't touch.

If you got on a bus, the body odor was bad and tourists thought the Russians were unhygienic. The truth was that they couldn't get soap. This was in the communist days when Russians would carry string bags and if they saw a line, they'd get in it. It didn't matter what was being sold, they knew they needed it, and a sliver of soap was very precious. It's hard to stay clean without soap.

The big ship's tour in St. Petersburg was to the Hermitage Museum, which housed the Tzar's collection of art. It was amazing, with rooms full of Rembrandts, Van Goghs and every other famous artist. We entertainers could get free tours by riding on the tour buses and counting passengers when they got on and off. It only took me two years to realize it was easier to count the empty seats. Duh.

But at the Hermitage, it was a people zoo. Loads of buses from different ships and people wandering in all directions. There was no way people were going to find the right bus so we just assumed they found one of ours and made it back. They always did.

If you spent a minute looking at every piece of art in that Museum it would take something like two years to get through. Dave Coleman, my Seattle drummer friend, and I

Mike Neun

made it through in 45 minutes. Well, we'd been there many times and it has to be said we were the world's worst art lovers.

One more Dave Coleman story. We were on a Seabourn ship going up the Amazon and we stopped in Belem, Brazil. We didn't know it, but Belem was a tough town with a very poor population and lots of crime. Smart tourists research these things, Dave and I just hopped off the ship and started walking. We always walked in any direction hoping to find adventure or at least a coffee shop.

So we walked for awhile and we noticed there weren't a lot of people on the sidewalks. It was very quiet. Suddenly we were surrounded by four guys, one of whom had a rusty old kitchen knife about 10 inches long. When I later told the story on stage, that knife turned into a razor-honed machete. They started going for our pockets and Dave was fighting them off. I realized this was a really bad idea and told him to just give them the money and we did. Then, like smoke, they vanished.

A few seconds later a woman drove up and said she saw what had happened. She drove us to the police station. They asked us what the muggers looked like and we were useless. We had no idea what they looked like. We agreed they weren't Asian. The police rolled their eyes.

The lady gave us a ride back to the ship and once there we discovered we weren't the only victims. Other crew members had gotten robbed, with some of them forced to lie on the ground while the muggers took everything they had.

Ah, but there was one bright spot. On board the ship we had a security officer who was kind of a dick. He was a retired British cop and he bullied the crew. Definitely a dick. Well, he was standing beside the ship taking video and a guy raced up, ripped off his gold watch, jumped into the river and swam away. It's not often you root for a thief, but this one had a lot of fans.

Let me be clear. I worked the ships for twenty years and loved all the ports, even Belem. I walked everywhere and only felt threatened two or three times. You can get mugged in the U.S. just as easily as any other country in the world, so take a trip. See the world. It'll blow your mind.

On another trip up the Amazon, Paul McFarland and I found a guy with a boat who promised to show us piranhas and black caiman crocodiles. It was a great tour. We fished for piranhas and that is a whole new ballgame. You know how you normally fish? Where you sit quietly in the boat and try not to spook the fish? Piranha fishing is just the opposite. You bait the hook with meat and then swirl it around in the water. The piranhas attack and you yank the hook out with a piranha attached and flip him into the canoe. Then you dance around trying to get away from those razor-sharp teeth as it flops around in the bottom of the boat. It's both exciting and silly, as I think the only use for the fish is to stuff it and sell it to tourists. I'm sure it's not edible, but I could be wrong.

The amazing part is while we were catching piranhas there were Brazilian kids swimming in the river about 30 yards from us.

Then it got dark and we went looking for crocodiles. This consisted of motoring near the shore and shining a flashlight. If there were crocodiles, the light would reflect off their eyes and the guy told us if the eyes were wide apart it was time to make a run for it.

It was a great tour until it came time to go back to the ship and he couldn't get the outboard motor started. This was serious stuff, because if we missed the ship it could cost us our jobs. He kept pulling on the starter rope, all the while pushing the choke button in and out. It was then we looked over and saw the choke button wasn't attached to anything. We also saw that instead of the sparkplug having a cap on it with a wire leading out, he had just stripped the insulation and wrapped the wire around the top of the plug. I'm no mechanic but I don't think that's a really good connection. We all fiddled with the engine and eventually got it started. That's how Paul and I didn't end up living on the Amazon selling piranhas to tourists.

Once on a Seabourn cruise we sailed further up the Amazon and stopped at a deserted island. The cooks and crew prepared a barbecue for the guests and we all motored over in tenders for a big party on the island. In time, some native kids swam over and hesitantly approached a bunch of us entertainers and dancers. Wow, we thought, we are interacting with people who have never seen civilization. This is a special moment. Then someone put on music and the kids lit up and said, "Michael Jackson!"

That's when I knew the true meaning of stardom. If you're famous in the jungle a thousand miles up the Amazon, you've hit the big time.

HITTING THE LANGUAGE WALL

If you decide to retire and live your life in Thailand you should learn to speak the language, right? Well I thought so too and when I got to Chiangmai I signed up for language lessons at AUA, a language school in the center of town.

I didn't care about reading and writing Thai, I just wanted to speak the language and I applied myself. Over the next three years I studied there and the YMCA and I took lessons from two tutors, both of whom were excellent.

The first was a young college guy named Tanapong and he would come to my apartment and give me lessons. I learned bits and pieces of Thai culture from him. I learned the Pizza delivery boys bought their own motorbikes and earned very little money. I learned that Thai people get food poisoning occasionally from street food. I thought it was just us foreigners. One day my closet door was open and he was amazed at how many shirts I had. I felt greedy.

One day, the owner of the apartment and his wife came in my door unannounced while Tanapong and I were sitting at my table studying Thai. They said they had to check the air conditioning but that seemed really bogus. Tanapong asked if they'd ever done that before and I said no and thought it was strange. We then realized they thought I was some old gay guy corrupting Thai teenagers and they were going to break it up.

Tanapong was a great teacher and I tried hard but when he wanted to take me to a market so I could talk with Thai people I couldn't do it. Too shy.

I learned a lot of words. I learned how sentences were constructed. I learned that the Thai language is a language of tones and that a word can have five different meanings depending on the tone. I learned that Thai and English are extremely difficult languages to learn and after three years of study, including listening to Thai music in the car and Thai news at home, I still could not speak or understand Thai.

I hit the wall, and quit. I know now I should've kept going. But I also know that lessons, grammar and learning words are not the best way to learn a language. The best way is to be an extrovert, love talking to people, and even better, work alongside them. My friend Derek Schade is a golf pro and he's spent years working with Thai people. He speaks excellent Thai. My wife, a pretty stern critic of foreigners who think they speak good Thai, says Derek speaks it well.

However, if you're not gregarious and would rather read books than socialize, you are at a huge disadvantage. I think this holds true of all countries and all languages. I have friends who drink way too much and they speak much better Thai than I do because they spend their nights talking to Thai bartenders and bargirls. Jintana calls it "bar Thai" and apparently it's kind of low class but at least they can speak something.

I can speak golf Thai. I know the words for left, right, straight ahead, up, down, sand trap, water hazard, hole, and the names of all the clubs. When I first got here the caddies called hybrids "Kathoeys", which is the Thai word for ladyboys. It makes sense because hybrids are neither woods or irons but somewhere in between.

Mike Neun

I still know lots of words, but when I use them Jintana's nieces roll their eyes and laugh because my pronunciation is awful. They can say a word looking me full in the face, I will repeat what they said exactly as I heard it, and they will laugh. Not even close.

Jintana speaks English very well and while that makes life easy for me I wonder if I would've learned Thai if that were all she spoke. Also, the kids have been taking English in school for years and they still have trouble with it. Because we use it a lot around the house I'm sure they're ahead of a lot of their friends but I'm realizing how very hard it is to learn a language.

I never should've quit the classes. I should've forced myself into social situations with Thai people. I'm a college graduate for Christ's sake. I'm not stupid. But I hit the wall.

Now, let's talk about all those people who say, "If you're going to live in America you'd better speak English." They are violent about it and they look down on immigrants who either can't speak it or speak broken English. I would've been one of those immigrants.

Let's look closer.

If you're an immigrant, what is the usual pattern? If you're Barbara Yoshida's parents, you are poor and you work like dogs long hours every day. Many immigrants hold down two or three low-paying jobs just to put food on the table. Where do they get the time or the money to study English? Can you give them the five or ten years it takes to learn a language, or are you going to sneer at them and tell them to go back where they came from?

That is why the pattern of immigrants is one where the parents have trouble with the language and the kids pick it up. That's how it works. The kids go to school, study the language, and hang out with kids who speak it. So maybe we should cut immigrants a little slack. Let them learn English as best they can and let them speak their own language among friends and family. Their kids will learn English. It's the pattern and it's not a bad one.

I'm an immigrant and the perfect example of the old joke. What do you call someone who is monolingual?

An American.

That's me, unless I'm playing golf.

Mike Neun

IF I HAVEN'T OFFENDED YOU WITH POLITICS, RELIGION SHOULD DO IT

I'd just retired and was on my flight to Bangkok to start my new life. Wouldn't you know it, seated next to me was a beautiful Thai woman and I thought, this has to be an omen. I'm sure she's looking to hook up with an old guy recovering from prostate surgery and radiation. We began talking and I immediately put my foot in it.

"Why are you moving to Thailand?" she asked.

I listed some reasons, and one of them was to get away from Christians. It turned out she was on her way back to Thailand to help run a Christian orphanage. Oops.

The truth was I was tired of in-your-face evangelical Christians and was looking forward to living in a Buddhist country. I am not a Buddhist, but if I had to choose that is the path I would probably follow. I'm not much of anything, really.

When we were kids we went to church on Sundays. In Detroit I think we were Methodists but those memories are very hazy. I remember being in a big gray church singing songs and saying prayers.

When we move to Grosse Ile we became Episcopalians because that was the only protestant church on the island and it was a good one. The minister, Archie Crowley, was a kind, gentle man and everyone loved him. Towards the end of our time there he moved up in the church and a new, more forceful minister took over. I'm sure it wasn't easy following in Rev. Crowley's footsteps but we didn't like the new guy as much.

The church had a basketball court out back and we played hours of pickup games there. It wasn't far from our house and I would ride my bike over to play. I can remember shoveling snow off that court to play in the winter so I guess we were dedicated.

I also remember being an acolyte. I would put on a long maroon cassock and then a white surplice and we would march down the aisle with one of us holding the cross in front. Russel Brad became famous for tripping one Sunday and breaking the cross off the pole. I became famous for kneeling at the altar during morning prayer and peeling off in a dead faint. Morning prayers were a bit long.

In 1957 we left Grosse Ile to move to Seattle. It was one of the great moments in my life because Seattle was a totally different culture from Michigan. Seattle is a university town with three or four colleges and the thinking seemed much more open to me. Then too, I was just starting my college career at the University of Washington. My church going days were over and my beer drinking days had begun.

At first I was totally overwhelmed. I had come from a high school with about 200 kids to a University with 17,000 students. I just walked around bumping into things.

Religion popped up in two different ways. At one point I took a class in the Bible as literature. I took it because the professor was renowned for interesting lectures and that was true. Sadly, I took it at one o'clock in the afternoon and

Mike Neun

was generally sleepy after lunch and my bridge game in the Commons, but the lectures were really good and I learned a lot about the stories in the Bible. I have since forgotten them all. Retention is for wimps.

My second experience was reading Jack Kerouac and Ken Kesey books, which introduced me to Buddhist thinking. These were the beatnik writers and there was all kinds of Zen stuff being talked about. I then moved into books like *Zen and the Art of Archery, Siddhartha,* and *Zen and the Art of Motorcycle Maintenance.* Buddhist thought made a huge amount of sense to me.

Here's my quick comparison of Christianity and Buddhism:

In Christianity, you are born a horrible person. A sinner. Christ died for you because you are so awful. And your only hope for salvation is to spend your life praying for forgiveness.

In Buddhism, you are born a good person and your job is to meditate and try to find that goodness inside you.

Tough choice.

I loved the Zen idea of doing something to the point where it becomes absolutely simple and pure. *Zen and the Art of Archery* became my blueprint for sports, music and comedy. I can honestly say I seldom found that pure simplicity but it was worth the effort. I've also meditated sporadically over the years and never achieved inner peace. I do think I'm a little more calm than I would've been, but I'm not a real Buddhist.

In college, my real religion was folk music and beer, not necessarily in that order, and I pursued them both with great dedication. I also joined a fraternity and in one of the worst decisions of my life helped start the Thursday Night Drinking Society. It was a loose group and a stupid idea because most of the tests were on Fridays. We lowered a lot of grade points.

I loved drinking. All my life I'd tried to say and do the right thing and beer gave me the freedom to blurt out stuff I'd never dream of saying in public. I went from an uptight striver to a drunken rebel and loved every minute of it with the possible exception of hangovers. All my life I've suffered monumental hangovers because I figured if one or two beers were good, twenty would be awesome. Also, when drinking I became a mad scientist of alcohol. What if you mixed beer and vodka? How about tequila with a gin chaser? I'm tired of Guinness, let's try Sambuca. That last one was from a wild night in Dublin, Ireland, with some musicians from the cruise ship and resulted in the worst hangover of my life.

As you can see, my religious studies took a long, hard sidetrack.

Those party days grew tiring and I also saw a lot of friends fall by the wayside, done in by liquor and drugs. I don't think I was an alcoholic but I was pushing the envelope and one day I just quit drinking. I didn't drink for about twenty years, and that was a good decision.

When I retired I figured I'd do all the stuff I'd missed along the way and LSD was at the top of the list. It was a fun dream but somehow I grew wiser and realized that the people who make drugs in garages and trailer parks are probably not at the top of the scientific food chain. I don't trust the drugs to be what they're cracked up to be and I don't trust the people who sell them. In Jamaica, when the ships would dock, the drug sellers would team up with the police. They'd sell you a baggie of marijuana, then the police would swoop in, arrest you, give the baggie back to the dealer, and you'd be off to jail. Hard to trust people like that.

Mike Neun

One time in Jamaica a friend of mine bought a baggie and brought it back to the ship. "Are you crazy?" I cried. "Haven't you heard about Jamaican jails? Haven't you heard about the police scams?"

He just laughed and set out to roll a joint. It turned out the grass he'd bought was just that. Grass. Clippings from a lawn mower. A sucker born every minute.

So I never achieved my dream of being a stoner geezer. I never had my mind expanded with LSD. And while I did drink a fair amount in Thailand, the hangovers have convinced me it's not worth the effort. Who would've dreamed I'd become a total lightweight? I could be a Baptist!

So. Religion. I think you should follow whatever you want to believe. I also think if you try to sell your religion to me our friendship will take a big hit. I don't believe in God and I don't think you have to believe in Him, or Her, to be a good person. Any idiot can figure out that it's wrong to murder people or steal or do things that hurt others.

I do believe in impermanence, living simply, trying to be a good person and trying to find some sort of inner peace. I think if you're going to have prayer in schools you should also teach math in church. It's only fair.

P.S. You cannot meditate your way to hitting a flop shot to an elevated green. You have to practice. Amen.

FAMILY VALUES, AND HOW TO OVERCOME THEM

I feel I have shortchanged my dad and mom. Here is more.

Both of my parents graduated near the top of their class at Wayne University. My mom came from a well-to-do family, members of the Detroit Yacht Club. I remember going there with my grandparents and seeing the beautiful wooden boats and elegant clubhouse with billiard tables and dark wood paneling and leather chairs. Her family name was Skinner and her father was a gentle guy who smoked a pipe.

My dad's background was different. His father had a dental repair service. My dad helped him and they repaired all kinds of dental equipment, including X-ray machines. My dad figured he'd gotten more than his share of radiation. His father was a little man and known to have a violent temper. He had a Model A pickup truck with a steel back bumper and once someone cut him off on the road. He pulled back around the guy, got in front and slammed on the brakes. Messed up that car.

My dad worked harder than I ever did. He worked for Detroit Power Screwdriver Company and he also taught business at Wayne University night school. On weekends he would help out in the dental repair business. At one point he bought a Crosley, a tiny little car and rebuilt the engine in our garage. Mom used it to drive me and other kids home from basketball practice and I was embarrassed. The other kids thought it was fun. My dad had a metal lathe in the basement and machined stuff with it. He also had a drill press. At one point he and Mom took classes in how to make jewelry and they made stuff out of silver.

Mom was always trying new things. At one point in Detroit she found a place where they played polo and you could go watch for free. There were two kinds of polo. The outdoor game was played on a huge field and it was hard to see. The indoor game wasn't indoors but in a smaller sort of a stadium. We liked that better.

Mom also got us to try skiing and it wasn't easy. We didn't want to go. Later it became a huge part of life for all of us. When he was about 70, that's how Dad discovered he had a form of Parkinson's Disease. He was standing in a lift line, ready to go up the mountain, and fell over for no reason.

As a little kid I went to Dad's plant a couple of times and it was like Disneyland for me. Big pulleys along the ceiling with leather belts running down to power the machines. Punch presses, lathes, all kinds of noisy machinery with men running them. My dad was in management, but I thought the plant floor was far more exciting than his office.

In 1957 he had a chance to go into a new business in Seattle, selling hydraulic pumps and valves with two partners. It was a huge decision because he'd been in the Detroit company over 20 years, but he and Mom went for it.

Mom, always inventive, hired an auction company to come sell all the stuff we couldn't take with us. I remember

Mike Neun

them saying they lost money on the big stuff but made a surprising amount on little things.

We drove to Seattle to join Dad's two new partners. Dad had only met one of them and liked him a lot. Halfway across the country we got word that that guy had gone boating in the Pacific Ocean and was lost at sea. So now Dad was on his way to go into business with Charlie Fisher, the partner he'd never met. Talk about stressful!

Luckily, Charlie was a great guy and it worked out but being a sales rep. was a very difficult job for Dad. He told me sometimes he'd wait outside a company for a half hour or more, building up the courage to go in and try to sell his hydraulic equipment.

I remember one time there was a convention and my dad came up with a display that was simple and really effective. He designed a series of tracks connected with pumps and valves and made a block of wood with the company name painted on it. The block would ride down a track, stop, get turned around, and pushed down another track. At every stop it would get flipped over or turned and at the end it would get lifted up to start over. People were entranced by it.

My dad was successful and deserved it because he worked hard at everything he did. We had a good, middle class life. Not rich, but okay.

In high school I worked summers at a golf course. In college I had summer jobs and also worked after classes. For a year or so I made pizza and washed dishes at Pizza Pete's. I also got fired.

The job was interesting because we'd work late and people would come in for pizza after the bars closed. I guess it was my destiny to work with drunks. One night a man and a woman came in yelling at each other. They argued all the time we made their pizza and then then took it outside and other customers came in saying they were having a huge argument outside. Then the woman came back in and we were horrified. It looked like blood all over her face and we thought he'd beaten her up. Then she got closer and we realized it was pizza sauce and anchovies. He'd thrown the pie in her face. We helped her as best we could.

I did just fine at Pizza Pete's until a new manager came in. He realized it didn't take three of us to run the place, so we'd take turns heading out for an hour or two while the other guys covered. He also introduced us to moose milk, a glass of milk with a couple shots of scotch in it. We were fucking up. One night I went to get a pizza out of the oven but missed. The paddle slipped over the crust and shoved all the topping into the back of the oven. It was a huge, smoking mess.

What we didn't know was that Pete, the owner, would send in spotters. These were people who acted like customers but reported back to him on what the employees were doing. Uh oh.

One night he came in with a new crew and fired us. He was right to do so but I blame the moose milk.

One of my parent's friends worked at Union Oil and one summer he got me a job in their warehouse. On the first day the foreman, who was 50 years old and weighed about 160 pounds, tipped a full barrel of oil on edge and rolled it on the rim over to a bunch of other barrels. Then he told me to do it and I noticed the other workers glancing over. No big deal, I thought, and tried to tip the barrel on edge. Not a chance. It was like trying to move a post. Guys were laughing and I heard remarks about smart young college kids. I kept yanking on that thing to no avail until the foreman took pity and showed me how to do it. You have to grab it on top, put your foot against the bottom and then throw all your weight backwards. Also, you have to stop it from tipping completely over, which would be really embarrassing. I got the hang of it after awhile.

Mike Neun

I also learned to drive a fork lift. Did you know you can duplicate a bad pizza error with a forklift and a pallet full of cases of oil? Here's how. First you get overconfident and drive too fast. Then you lift up the pallet full of cases of oil and zip over to the truck that's backed up to the loading dock. You blithely speed up to the truck, not noticing that your forks are a little low and prang them into the back of the truck. You then watch with horror as all those cases of oil fly into the truck and the cans burst open.

There is no good way to clean up oil. You just get lots of rags and spend a day mopping it up. Once again there were murmurs about smart college kids.

I also got to work the canner. This was a conveyor machine that canned oil. On one end you took boxes of empty cans, tipped them onto the belt and made sure they were all right side up. That was the job. It was mind-numbing work and I learned that I liked numbing my mind. It was meditative, and after a couple of hours I would feel surprisingly calm.

I noticed that at Pizza Pete's too, washing dishes. We did them by hand, and I found I liked it. Later in life I realized if comedy failed, I could always be a dishwasher.

I learned there is no such thing as a demeaning job. You do what you have to do and you do it well. In time, if you follow that path, you will rise in your profession.

My dad taught me a respect for investing and taking care of money. Even when I was drinking and carousing I managed to put a little of my wages aside. I'd invest in mutuals funds, just a little bit of my money, and then forget it. I never traded stocks and I was warned very strongly about the dangers of commodity investing. Nope, just mutual funds. I invested the most when I was working cruise ships, because I was making good money and the expenses were minimal. I was never rich, but I had enough to retire when the time came.

You know what the biggest money move was? The one that put me in fat city? I never had kids. It's not a good way to go and I missed out on a lot of life's greatest joys. I just thought it wouldn't be fair to the kids. I never knew if I'd have a job two weeks down the road and I knew I would never be home to help raise them. It wouldn't be fair. Financially it saved me thousands, but I would never, ever, advise anyone to not have kids.

Now I live in Thailand. It's getting prosperous here but there are a lot of very poor people and foreigners are considered rich. I've never thought of myself as rich and it's weird. In the states I'd barely be middle class, but here I'm rich and I don't think I like it. I just want to be normal and have enough for green fees.

Mike Neun

WHY YES, I HAD A TV SHOW

Did I tell you I was a TV star? Well, first we should define "TV star." Some people think it means you were on national TV and you're a household name to millions of people. But even that has limits. I love Ellen Degeneres, but there are a billion people in China who have no clue who she is. Michael Jackson was famous in the jungles of the Amazon. So it's all relative.

I was famous in Spokane, Washington. When I did my PBS shows there, I was famous enough to fill a theater. If I'd done those shows in Los Angeles, we might've drawn 12 or 13 people. It's relative.

Also, time enters into it. Fifty years ago, all Americans knew who Dinah Shore was and knew about her TV shows. Now, you ask anyone under fifty and they will have no idea who she is. Well, I'll tell you. She was a famous singer, she was in love with Burt Reynolds (again, a meaningless name to people under fifty) and at one time she had a very popular daytime TV show. It was on that show that I learned you can use up ten years worth of material in four months. I was living in L.A. and got booked on her show. I did well, and got asked back. I kept getting asked back and in four months I'd used up all my A material, my B material, my on-a-good-night-this-might-work material, and was into my improv skills, which were nonexistent.

It was on this last-ditch, hang-by-my-fingernails mode that I got booked and her other guest was Richard Pryor. He was at the peak of his powers and he blew me out of the water. That was the end of that.

I also did a couple other network shows down there that you've never heard of. "The Norm Cosby Show" and "Live at the Improv." I did well. When I could do my A material, I was a class act. But I couldn't come up with A material quick enough for TV. It sucked it up and spit me out.

Ah, you say, but were you famous anywhere else?

Yes, for a couple of years I had my own TV show on the Canadian network, CBC, out of Vancouver, B.C.

I'd guested on some TV shows in Canada and apparently they thought I was ready to host a show. We did it in an in-the-round format and it was a good show because we had great guests. In Vancouver there was a huge nightclub called The Cave, and Las Vegas acts would come up to do a week to perfect their shows before taking them down to Vegas. (We big timers call it Vegas). So the Cave had some really big names pass through, and my producer, Ken Gibson, was really good at getting them to come on our show to help promote theirs.

I tried hard to be a good host. For one thing, I lobbied to have a cast of regulars on the show. I wanted to have a team to help carry the load and I still think it's a great idea. I wasn't the guy who wanted it all about me. So we got some local entertainers to be on with me every week. The big problem is I didn't know how to blend them in while I was dealing with guests, but I'm sure I could do it now if anyone wants an 80-year-old TV host. Push that envelope!

Ah, but the guests were great. Duke Ellington was the biggest prize and I was in awe. I tried to think of questions to ask him, like, "Have you ever thought of writing a Broadway show?" Luckily, I didn't ask because I found out later he'd done two or three already and they were famous. Oops. Happily he'd done thousands of interviews and just took off talking. Thank you, Mr. Ellington.

Another act that blew me away was the Mills Brothers. These guys had had some huge hits in the fifties and by the time they got on my show they were quite old. Also, one of them was nearly blind and had to be helped on stage. Wow, I thought, this might not be a good idea. Then they sang and it was glorious. Perfect harmonies, ultimate professionals, and so very, very smooth.

O.C. Smith was on my show, riding a huge hit song that I can't remember now. He was a great guest and afterwards he invited me to The Cave to see his show. We got there a little late and ended up sitting in the balcony. In the middle of his show he stopped and said, "I had a great time doing a TV show today and the host is here tonight. Let's hear it for Mike Neun!" I stood up and nobody noticed! I couldn't figure out what the hell was going on. No spotlight, nothing. I found out later that a fellow entertainer, Terry David Mulligan, had stood up on the ground floor and taken my bow, waving and laughing to the audience.

Then we come to a real downer. Rolf Harris was on my show. At the time he was riding high on a couple of hit songs and was a good guest. We played harmonicas together, talked, he sang a song and drew a cartoon. An all-around performance. Years later it came out that he was a pedophile and got sent to prison. So I can say I had Rolf Harris on my TV show and opened in Tahoe for Bill Cosby. If I'd been assaulted by Harvey Weinstein I could've had the evil trifecta.

Our show lasted for a couple of years. I gained about twenty pounds. Another lesson, never choose an apartment next to an Italian bakery. I'm a sucker for any kind of bread and theirs was out of this world.

As a side note, I just remembered another of my college jobs was washing dishes in a cheesecake bakery in Seattle. Once it gets out that you're a world-class dishwasher, the opportunities are endless. It was run by a Swiss gentleman and his product was used by the best restaurants in town. He made it in round metal molds, and my process was to run my finger around the mold, lick up the bits of cheesecake, and wash the mold. Again, a solid weight-gain technique.

The Canadian show was first called "In The Round," then changed to "Neun at Night." We had two good years and life was just fine. The show was successful but Ken Gibson, our producer, was a lover of pop music and big production shows. He wanted to make our show like that, and the next year we took our first show to a big auditorium and filled the stage with singers and dancers. All I remember is that about 30 people showed up to see it, and it bombed. I'd asked to bring in my old partner, Brian Bressler, for the show because I wanted to give him a Canadian shot and because again TV had sucked up every bit of material I'd ever come up with. We tried hard to make it work, but it came off as a big production show in an empty room and it failed. That was the end of my show in Canada.

Fame. It is relative, it is fleeting, it is fickle, and it's a lousy goal. Luckily I learned early that the best goal is to try to do good work and see where it takes you. Sometimes, because of your own limitations, you can't do good work. Sometimes you're at the mercy of others, or bad situations, or lousy microphones, or drunken idiots in a bar crowd. All you can do is keep going. The good news is I always had a fallback plan. I was a world-class dishwasher.

Mike Neun

HA HA DEATH, I LAUGH AT YOU

L et's cheer things up now and talk about death. In Thailand
they cremate most dead people. There are Buddhist
monks who sit in the crematoriums and meditate on
death. I have chosen not to do that.

Back in 2003 I went in to see my old college buddy, Dr.
Glen Ruark, for a physical. He found my PSA was up around
17 and that's not a good thing. Then they did a biopsy and that
was painful. I was brave. Well, I didn't have a choice because
I didn't want Glen hearing me scream for my mommy. The
biopsy came back positive for prostate cancer. I learned that
if you're going to get cancer, prostate cancer is the way to
go. In the old days they didn't even treat it because it was
usually slow moving and you'd probably die from something
else first.

We went over the choices. Now there are lots more
options because medicine has made progress but back then
the operation seemed logical. If the cancer was confined to
the prostate, they could get it all and I'd get on with my life.
So I opted for that.

I have to admit I was fatalistic. None of this "Oh no, I'm
going to die!" panic for me. I figured I'd had a really good life
and whatever happened I was way ahead of the game.

They operated and they also took out a lymph node to see if the cancer had gotten out of the prostate. It had. A tiny amount had escaped. Damn those sneaky cancer cells.

I had the best recovery ever, because after the operation Glen and Judy invited me to stay at their farm outside of Spokane. I think it sets your mind at ease to recover in the home of a doctor and a registered nurse. You can't get better care than that. They were wonderful. As soon as I could, I got up and went for walks. In time I was back jogging. I'm a firm believer in exercise and because I'm also lazy I chose jogging as my exercise of choice. You can run a mile or two in under 20 minutes. Anyone can do 20 minutes a day.

The next step was radiation. I was living with my brother in Eugene, Oregon, at the time so I went to a cancer center there. I had some questions I wanted to ask the radiologist so I wrote them down and went in for the first appointment. He was a very prim guy with a bow tie and when I tried to ask the questions he just brushed me off. Apparently he was the God of medicine and I was some peon taking up his valuable time. I thought seriously of going somewhere else, but I don't think there were a lot of choices in Eugene. First they tattooed dots on my lower stomach to line up the machine and a male nurse assured me that the radiologist was the best and I was in good hands. I needed that. I did 8 weeks of radiation and there was some pain but other than that it was okay.

The hope was that the radiation would get the rest of the cancer, but it didn't.

When I recovered, I entered into a life-long routine of a hormone shot every three months. The shot keeps the testosterone down and testosterone carries the cancer. The downside is they are female hormone shots so I lost a lot of body hair (I don't hang out in locker rooms). Also the shots gave me hot flashes and mood swings. The mood swings were nothing new, I've always bounced around on the manic-

Mike Neun

depressive scale. One bad show and I'm dark as hell. A good show and I'm king of the world.

I still get those mood swings and had one yesterday. They are a bitch. I played golf in the morning and the switch in my brain clicked over. Suddenly I was mad at my swing, my partner, the weather, grass, trees, everything. I tried to keep quiet and soldier on but after 15 holes I told my friend the medicine was getting me and I had to go in. I decided to eat a big breakfast and go home, get in bed and watch Grey's Anatomy all day. It was a good plan, but I'd forgotten Jintana and I had promised to drive Awee to her singing lesson. That pissed me off too, and I was moody on the drive and while we waited for Awee. I'd told Jintana what was happening and tried very hard to just be quiet. We got back home and I went back to bed. Later I went out alone to dinner and found myself crying in the car. I got back home, went to bed and this morning was back to normal. Male menopause is a terrible thing.

Ah, and now the hot flashes. I am firmly on the side of every woman going through menopause. Hot flashes are a bitch. You're living your life and suddenly it feels like you're running a marathon in Saudi Arabia. If you're playing league golf in Thailand, where insanity rules, in the hottest part of the day and suddenly you get a hot flash you've just doubled down. Your legs buckle, all the energy drains from your body, a mood swing kicks in, and it seems only right to send your 6-iron helicoptering through the air. I could not handle that stuff at all, and I would just lose it. I'd be a nice guy for 14 or 15 holes and then bam, it was like a switch clicked in my brain and I was Attila the Hun. I lost friends. I was ashamed. I could not fix it.

Then an ex-police chief from California, Tony Giardino, taught me the joys of crack-of-dawn golf. Cool weather, an empty course all to ourselves, and 18 holes in less than

2 1/2 hours. He saved my golfing life. I was no longer a monster, except on very rare occasions when my game was so bad the mood swing switch clicked. Even then I wasn't quite the idiot I'd been before.

After I recovered from the operation and radiation—does it feel like were bouncing around in time?—I worked another couple of years on the cruise ships. But it was like the TV shows. I'd used up all my material and even though I was writing every day I wasn't coming up with new stuff. Also, I'd seen some ship entertainers who'd stayed too long and just weren't good anymore. I was feeling that about myself so I retired.

Back when I'd just had the operation I'd asked Glen to give me an honest answer about how long I could expect to live and he'd guessed around ten years. That was seventeen years ago, so I think Thailand has health properties a lot of people haven't discovered. Another thing is that a friend gave me the name of a great oncologist here, Dr. Chaiyut, and I'm convinced he's kept me alive much longer than expected.

So, death. I once wrote a death song because, hey, I like to think outside the box. You don't see a lot of comedians doing death material. So when it comes to dying I still feel the same way, that I've had a wonderful life and have no complaints. On top of that, the last 13 years with Jintana and her family have been like winning the lottery. Now I really, really have no complaints.

My main thought is that I don't want a long, lingering death. I like the eskimo idea of walking out into a blizzard. I think the Thai version of that would be to buy a Ducati, take it up to the mountains and open her up. Without a helmet of course. One tight curve at 90...problem solved.

Jintana and I have talked about death, because in Thailand people can spend a lot of money on a long funeral with chanting that can last for days. I want my funeral to be

Mike Neun

quick. Chant a little bit and then on to cremation. She's fine with that.

So, death, I laugh at you. You can't hurt me, and if by some outside chance the Christians are right and there's a heaven and hell, I don't think a guy who spent his life in bars and casinos is going to be heading upstairs. That's fine with me, because I know all my idols, the greatest musicians, comedians and authors, will be headed down too. That place will be rocking.

MORNING IN CHIANG MAI

Jintana and I were both awake at 4:30 a.m. and didn't know why. I don't sleep well because hot flashes wake me up once or twice a night. She usually can sleep through anything but occasionally she is wide awake for no reason.

Are you married? Do you have thermostat wars? In every marriage one person is always too hot and one is always too cold. It is the law. For years, I was always too hot and Jintana was always too cold. She is Thai and has lived her entire life in a hot country. In Thailand old people in the mountains freeze to death in temperatures that are normal in Seattle. In the summers here, temperatures get in the 40s and stay there. I don't know what that is in Fahrenheit, but I'm guessing you can cook pizzas on the sidewalks.

I lived most of my life in Michigan, Washington and Idaho. I have chipped ice off windshields and dug cars out of snow so waking up to sunshine every day is just fine with me. Oh sure, Thailand is too hot but I have found ways to adjust. I also have deep feelings for our air conditioner.

But now, things are reversing. Jintana is too hot and when the A.C. is on I'm too cold. She is nearly fifty years old and her body may be changing. It is no big deal, we will handle it. It is morning in Thailand.

In world news, the coronavirus has people edgy and Jintana has been stocking up on food. I read where this is a good idea, not just for a backup, but because in a pandemic even if you can go buy stuff you don't want to be in crowds of people at a supermarket and get exposed to the virus. I too bought a lot of my kind of food—granola and nuts, stuff like that. I assume the next move is to dig a bunker in the back yard and load up on AK-47s. We Americans know how to overreact.

I normally drive Kadjang to school three days a week and this is one of those days but she wants to go later because she has a test and doesn't have to be there at the normal time, around 7:30. Today it's a half hour later. Jintana will take Awee and we will meet, kind of, for breakfast. The times don't work out so I'll get to Butter is Better just as Jintana is finishing her meal. Not a big problem.

I have a couple hours to kill so I watch Grey's Anatomy on Netflix. Eleven years ago, when Jintana was living with me in my apartment, we got hooked on that show and watched the first few seasons on DVDs. Remember DVDs? Now the last few seasons are on Netflix and we're hooked again but we watch separately on our iPads. We don't have a TV set in our room. We used to, but the cable fees for two sets—one for her mom and one for us—were getting ridiculous.

You can get black boxes here that will bring in hundreds of channels and a friend put one in but our satellite wi-fi was undependable and the shows kept freezing. Nothing like watching a really close playoff game go into the last three minutes and having the TV freeze up. Also, with the old TV I would plug in headphones and watch while Jintana slept. We bought a new, big-screen TV and then discovered there was no way to use headphones. No output for a jack and no bluetooth connection. Crazy. So we gave the TV to Jintana's sister and her husband and just watch Netflix and YouTube

Mike Neun

on our iPads. I don't miss TV, and I really don't miss the commercials.

Jintana is cleaning the bathroom now. She is a fanatic about cleanliness. I'm a guy. If she didn't do it, I would but not as well. Now she comes over and stands with her back to me. Being a quick thinker I realized her dress has a bow in the back and she wants me to tie it. I do, not quite perfectly but close enough. I think of buying her flowers today for no reason. I haven't done that in a long time but it feels right.

I sit in my recliner chair with a pillow at the small of my back, my feet up on the bed and keyboard in my lap. It is my writing position. I read that Hemingway stood up when he wrote. I play golf, therefore I have back pain and need a recliner. A few months ago the pain was severe. I would stand up wrong, or roll over wrong, and it would feel like someone drove a spike into my lower back. I did what any smart person would do. I changed my golf swing and bought blow-up pillows for my car and chair to support my lower back. That worked. I get tiny twinges now but they are just reminders of the bad old days.

We sit, waiting for the kids to get ready. I write, Jintana watches her shows on Netflix.

Later today I will have lunch with Todd Sawyer and Randy Thompson. What are the odds that three ex-comedians from Seattle would end up living in Chiangmai? Todd is trying to make it now as a writer. Randy is retired and traveling the world. I am retired and have no desire to ever step into an airport again. Who would've thought plane travel would be more uncomfortable than buses?

We will talk politics, show business, Todd's recent marriage to a hill tribe lady and sports. Both Randy and Todd played baseball and I think Todd played basketball too. I never liked baseball but I do have one great memory. I must've been about 10 or 12 years old when my dad wrote a funny note to my teacher saying I had to go attend a funeral at Briggs Stadium. We went to see the Detroit Tigers play the Cleveland Indians and my first memory is how beautifully green the playing field was. Then, in maybe the 8th inning, my dad said, "Remember this, because you're watching history." There was huge round of applause and Satchel Paige, the legendary Black pitcher, walked to the mound. He must've been fifty years old, but Bill Veeck, the Indian's owner and consummate showman, had brought him up to the majors. He pitched an inning and I could be one of the few people alive who ever saw Satchel Paige pitch.

Randy, Todd and me. Randy did a bunch of acting on TV shows so he's pretty well set financially but he is still dying to do something. Todd is trying to sell scripts to movie studios and before last Christmas had what seemed like a firm offer. He is struggling and this would've been huge for him but Hollywood is cruel and it fell through. We were playing golf the day the offer came in and he was on the phone all through the game trying to get it finalized. They put him off for almost two months and then the deal crashed. Sometimes show business sucks.

We will go to the Bagel House. It's run by a couple of really nice Thai ladies. I'm guessing they are lesbians but my gaydar is wildly faulty so they could have husbands and tons of kids.

I still have an hour before Kadjang is ready for school. Grey's Anatomy beckons. I will write more later and hopefully I'll come up with something really exciting. I've already told you about the two fights in my life, both pretty tame, so I don't think this book is going to be made into an action flick. I hope Tom Cruise isn't depending on me.

Mike Neun

EMPTY BRAIN SYNDROME

If it weren't for mystery novels, I never would've made it through life. Also, I can honestly say I never figure out who the culprit was. I'm always surprised when the best friend or the kindly nun turns out to be an ax murderer. I think *gullible* is the word I'm looking for.

It's nighttime here in Chiangmai and people are worried about the coronavirus. In my lifetime there have been so many threats to the world—nuclear war, fascism, communism, terrorism, WW II, Korea, Vietnam, polio, rogue asteroids, earthquakes, tsunamis, etc.—that I have become kind of immune. It's like I've been vaccinated against disaster and it no longer affects me until the moment an asteroid obliterates the planet. There could definitely be a pandemic and this could be it, but it's like Donald Trump. It came, I could do nothing about it, so I'll get on with my life. I doubt if I'll take any trips to China though.

The big thing here in Chiangmai is that it's killing a lot of businesses. Thailand is a big tourist destination for the Chinese and the virus has dried that up completely. Our winter is wonderfully cool and mild and it is the high season for tourism. People come from all over the world to tour, hit the beaches, play golf, and buy stuff. It starts in late September and ends around March. Well, it's ending early this year and low season is going to be extra tough on Thai people. The good news is that Thai people handle adversity really well.

This morning we woke up at 6 a.m. and the plan was to take Jintana to breakfast and then to a friend's house. She and four of her old school classmates are going to a funeral in Lampang. I think it will be a very social trip for them. We tried some new drip coffee (my cutting back was just a fantasy) and it seemed quite strong. I also realized I have lost all my taste buds and can't really tell good coffee from bad. This means I can go to the local shops and get a cappuccino for 50 baht—under two dollars. One shop has it for 25 baht, which is under a dollar. I love Thailand.

We drove into town to Butter is Better and had our usual—a waffle and a fruit plate. We split all our breakfasts because it's just too much food. Jintana told me she was fat when she was younger but I've seen pictures of her in college and she wasn't what we Americans call fat. I've been on cruise ships and I know what real fat is. She was a bit overweight back then and didn't like it so she changed her diet.

My bad back won't let me jog any more so I have to watch what I eat. The stationary bike helps, but it's not the same.

I took her to her friend's house but they'd gone out to get something so we waited in the car. I watched Formula 1 on Netflix, which is a really good documentary series and very exciting. Once again I was thankful I no longer had to face the stress of competition. I watched the drivers prepare for races and realized it was about the same as standing backstage waiting to do a show. I also realized that a driver stuck in a bad car was the same as me going out in a bad venue with lousy sound and lights. You knew you weren't going to be great and you just had to do the best you could. As always, I rooted for the underdogs.

Mike Neun

When Jintana's friends got there I drove out to M-Sport driving range. M-Sport is an energy drink and the driving range is weird because they have huge, transformer-like statues out front built of gears and metal parts. I have no idea how they relate to golf, but the range is good and the people are nice.

I was waiting for the girl to bring the two trays of balls when I saw my Saturday golf buddy, New Orleans Joe, a few mats down.

I have spent years around golf professionals and like all amateurs, I feel I can spot flaws in other people's swings. This is a disease, it's lethal, and it's contagious. It it why you see guys shooting 95 telling other guy's what's wrong with their swing. It's really stupid and we've all done it. I have worked years to try to keep my mouth shut and damn it's hard. I say this because it's obvious to me that Joe takes the club back so far inside that he gets stuck and can't hit the ball without flipping the club and chasing the shot. Today I watched him make that move and it was killing me not to talk. But yesterday I shot 95. I sucked, and there are days when Joe beats me with that flawed swing. Hell, there are days when Ronald McDonald could beat me. So in my mind I'm thinking, "Just shut up, Mike. Work on your own stuff."

I failed. But I didn't say anything. Instead I stood behind him and took video. Then I messaged it to him and he saw the problem himself.

Golf is hard, because when you make a change it feels awful. You've grooved your mistake and the cure feels like a horrible move. I know, because a few months ago I took video of my swing and immediately saw a couple of major flaws. When I correct them, it feels like I'm swinging an axe. Hence the expression, "Feel isn't real."

In life, we all do the same thing. We make the same mistakes over and over and the corrections feel very strange.

I see people who talk way too much and have no clue that they're doing it. Hell, I might be one of them. I know I spent a couple of weeks trying to speak less and it was a revelation. I do talk too much!

I think a lot of people fail for those reasons. Change feels wrong. It's hard to do. Much easier to stay in your rut and wonder why other people are more successful. In my job, audiences let you know immediately if you were screwing up and that was a good thing. There was no mercy. If you did bad shows, you knew immediately. You had to change or die.

Years ago I read about opera singers, where someone tried to find the difference between the big stars and the mediocre singers. You know the surprising result? Volume. Not loudness, but the differences in volume. Great opera singers went from very soft to very loud and back again. Mediocre opera singers didn't vary their volume as much.

I learned that on bad nights on stage. When you get scared, you move towards a monotone. You close up when you should be opening up.

And you can err in both directions. The worst teacher I had in high school just had one volume. Loud. It was flat-out boring. Shy people talk softly, and become uninteresting because they never pump up the volume. Check out the great rock anthems, and I think you'll find they go from very quiet to very loud. "Stairway to Heaven" and "Bohemian Rhapsody" spring to mind.

This is a hard day of writing for me because my mind is all over the place. Awee, Jintana's niece, knocked and came in for a few minutes. She is the most cheerful person I've ever been around and I needed that. She doesn't walk, she dances, and finds joy in all things. She's gone now and it's like a light went out of the room. What a good little interlude that was.

What makes a good show? You know, for thousands of years people have been putting on plays, concerts, dances,

Mike Neun

and let's think of the venues that have evolved. Theaters. Theaters have generally the same shape, with a stage, a bunch of seats facing the stage, maybe balconies with seats facing the stage, and lighting that lights up the stage while the rest of the theater is dark. For me a theater with good sound and lights was perfect. I used to love being on stage with a spotlight on me, the audience in darkness, a great sound system and good acoustics. I loved having the light in my eyes because I didn't want to see the audience, I wanted to hear them and feel them. I wanted to get inside my material and not be distracted. I loved theater shows.

You know what's the opposite of a theater? A TV studio. Somewhere back in time a TV mogul said, "Let's design a big room with the most distractions we can think of and see if the entertainers can overcome them. Let's put TV cameras between the entertainer and the audience and have them move around and get in the way of any link between the performer and the studio audience. Oh, and yes, let's find some really bright lights! We need those crowd shots so let's light it so it's like doing a show at Walmart! And to make it even harder, let's make sure every act just does a really short amount of time. We don't want anyone building up rapport. Now, can we think of other distractions? How about random people in headsets scurrying around the cameras? Yes! I like it!"

I know. The studio audience is not your audience. The real audience is out there in TV land, watching you through the cameras and you have to play to them. Even so, I found it incredibly hard to focus on TV shows. I don't think I ever got inside my material the way I did in theater situations. I never, ever, felt the zen-like zone I sometimes found in theaters. The material always felt diminished.

So for me, doing TV was a lot like driving in Thailand. Things were coming at you from all directions and it was very confusing. I can do both, but it's more a matter of survival than bliss.

There is another venue that is just awful and that's a fairgrounds. There is nothing less exciting than doing a show where the stage is on the infield and the grandstand is across the racetrack. You have no idea what the crowd is doing because you can't hear them. So you just leave spaces and hope. Survival entertainment.

Speaking of survival, I once opened for Andy Williams on a tour of those in-the-round theaters back east. Before the first show, Andy did a long sound check and when it came to my turn the sound guy asked me what I needed. I said a voice mic and a guitar mic and asked if we'd do my sound check now. He said no need for that, we've got you covered.

So that night I got introduced, walked on stage, and neither microphone worked. No sound at all. 2,500 people yelling, "We can't hear you!" So I just stood there like a dumbass while the sound guys raced around sorting it out. For months I had dreams of standing on stage with people yelling at me while the sound guy said, "Don't worry, we've got you covered."

Yes, even theaters aren't perfect.

I once opened for Dione Warwick at Wolftrap, which is a famous outdoor theater in Virginia. I have no idea why, but I was wearing a cream-colored suit and I walked out and had one of the best shows of my life. Gangbusters. I took my bow, ran off stage, and tripped over a monitor. I fell and rolled in the dust backstage, but got up unhurt and feeling good. Ah, but the audience yelled for more. I walked back out, covered in dirt, hair in all directions, and got a great laugh. Then I did a short song and ran off, carefully. Encores are tough.

I'm realizing as I write this that it's not impressive to drop names that people under 30 have never heard of. A smart person would've written this book 50 years earlier.

Mike Neun

I love minimalism. In shows I wanted a stool, two microphones, a dark theater and a spotlight. I know there are people who love spectacle and I think my all-time favorite version of that was the opening ceremony at the Olympics in London. I thought it was inventive and awesome. But it was not something I'd ever dream of doing. This feeling carries over in life. I'd rather have a small, good house than a mansion. I love looking at expensive cars—the Morgans are my current favorites—but I'm happy in an inexpensive, good car. I'm way happier in shorts and a tee shirt than I am in a tuxedo. I love to keep it simple.

Oh sure, when you drive up to the front entrance of Caesar's Palace in Las Vegas in a VW Beetle and say, "Hi, I'm the new opening act", people think you're weird.

WANT TO LEARN HUMILITY?
COME TO THAILAND

It took me awhile to realize that Thai people are really unimpressed when you tell them you had a career as a musician/comedian. For them, musicians are the people who do background cover songs in bars while everyone drinks and talks. Also, judging from the Thai TV shows I've seen, the comedy here is extremely broad and filled with sound effects. Kind of like The Three Stooges with bells and whistles going off on every punch line. It is changing, and there is a Thai comedian named Udom who is very good and a woman comic actor who's in all kinds of shows and reminds me of Carole Burnett. I'm sure there are more and that Thai comedy is improving but with my nonexistent language skills it's hard to watch a lot of Thai television. What makes it even harder is not having a TV.

Another problem is there are a lot of fine musicians in Thailand and compared to them I am limited. If there is a language problem, my songs and stories are met with blank stares and polite applause. I know this because I've sat in a few times in Chiangmai with very mixed results. I've written hours of material and songs and over here I've found that I only have one that works in a mixed-nationality open mic. It's the country song that I never thought of as an opener or closer, but it's big in Thailand. It's about a country singer who can't write country songs because his life is too good. His wife never leaves him, his kids don't have dread diseases, he doesn't lose all his money, his dog loves the mailman and so on.

So I can go sing in bars here, but after that song I'm stumped and it's not really worth it to drive into town, lug a guitar to a bar, and do five minutes.

I've also done four shows for the bridge club. Two of them went very well, one was a bust, and one was drowned out by a pile driver down the road.

My friend, Ross Shaffer, told me a story about a guy who got hired to do an outdoor show in the big yard behind a mansion. He told them he didn't do outdoor shows but they swore up and down they'd set everything up perfectly, with good sound and lights, etc. He agreed and when he arrived the setup was indeed perfect. A stage was set up on a huge lawn with a beautiful lagoon behind it. The soundcheck was great, the lights right, and when people were all seated, facing him, he walked out to do his show. That's when hundreds of frogs erupted into song. I'd never heard of a show being blown away by croaking.

I had a friend on the ships, George Sakellariou, who is one of the greatest classical guitarists I've ever heard. He also has a wry sense of humor and does wonderful concerts. One day he was home and his wife answered the phone. The guy on the other end wanted George to play at his wedding. She told him George was a concert guitarist and didn't do weddings, but the guy asked to speak to George anyway. George picked up the phone and the guy said, "Hi George, I'm Steve Jobs and I love classical guitar."

George played the wedding.

Mike Neun

Where was I? I remember now, Thailand. One of the open mics here is at a place called Yummies Pizza and I had a friend, Doug Moeller, visiting from Seattle. Doug had seen me do TV shows, casinos and theaters and we balanced that out when I brought him with me to Yummies Pizza and he watched me bomb. Oh sure, there was a large table in front of the stage filled with loud, drunken Germans who didn't understand what the hell I was doing, so I had an excuse, but Doug loves to remind me of how low I've fallen.

I also thought I would inspire Jintana's nieces to take up guitar and the game of golf. I would share my knowledge and be a far better teacher than the idiot parents who haunt driving ranges and music studios, yelling at their kids and teaching them all the wrong things.

How could the girls resist my love of golf and music? Well, they've resisted very well thank you. I've taken them to the driving range and they like whacking the balls around but they have no desire to play golf because it's played in the sun. You think Americans judge people by the color of their skin? Thai people are equally bad. To them, dark skin means you're a farmer or a hill tribe person and very low on the social scale. Every skin-care product in Thailand is loaded with whiteners and every Thai movie and TV star is lily white. I have tried to explain to the girls that skin color means nothing and that there are beautiful people of all races. They just look at me like I'm an idiot. So not only did I fail to communicate my love of golf and music, I also failed to combat prejudice in my own home.

I now spend my days looking for sunscreens and lotions that do not contain whiteners. I have always been the whitest guy at every beach and those things could push me into translucent.

As for music, when Awee was small I would bring out the guitar and she not only didn't care about music, she took great joy in hanging rows of finger picks and thumb picks on the strings. Kadjang got a ukulele and I tried to show her chords and songs but she found a Thai music teacher on the Internet and learned the song that starts, "I'm just a little bit caught in the middle..." She played and sang it beautifully in a school show. Then she put the ukulele back in the case and never took it out again. Instead, she is taking piano lessons. I feel like the football player whose son decides to be a ballet dancer. I am humbled.

Finally, in retirement I have learned that my career as a not-famous comedian does not dazzle people. Undaunted, I keep trying to slide it into conversations with strangers only to find they don't really care. All those years of thinking my career was wildly important and interesting are falling by the wayside and that's a good thing. I've realized that the happiest I've ever been is here in Thailand with Jintana. I never get stage fright either. If the kids don't laugh at my jokes I can handle it. Barely.

I also learned another important Thailand lesson. The best time to go to the Sunday Walking Street in Chiangmai is when the coronavirus scare has thinned out the tourist herd. I felt I hadn't connected with Thailand enough lately so I drove downtown, parked and walked to the Walking Street. I was surprised to find sparse crowds and I loved it. It's a huge open market and normally jammed.

Jintana was at the funeral in Lampang with her friends, so I just rambled past all the stalls at my own speed. I picked up an ear of hot corn on the cob from a vendor for 20 baht (about 60 cents) and decided that would be dinner as I had pigged out the day before. I split my time between looking at the stuff for sale and looking at the people walking. Now and then I would see a beautiful woman and realize immediately she must be on the lookout for a really, really old guy who was kind of sweaty and hadn't bothered to shave. Yeah, right.

I saw lots of tattoos. When I was a teenager it never would've occurred to me that tattoos would some day be a sign of hip rebellion. Back then the only people who got tattoos were sailors and soldiers and they were kind of a low-class thing. I think Frank Zappa nailed it when he said they were a permanent reminder of a temporary feeling, but obviously I am again out of step with the entire world.

I munched on my corn and put money in the can of a blind guy singing Thai songs. I always tip street musicians, knowing that but for a good manager and a few breaks that could've been me. George Sakellariou, my guitarist friend, and I once had a long talk about how we had no pride and if worse came to worse we'd be out on the street playing for quarters. Mark Nizer, perhaps the most inventive juggler I've ever seen, started on the streets and now plays big theaters.

I kept walking, getting hot and sweaty, and that's when I heard someone call my name. It was a new golf buddy from Montreal with his wife and another couple who'd just flown in from Vietnam. I wasn't up to meeting people in my unshaven, sweaty state, but that's the way it goes. We talked and they wanted to know about the tailor I'd recommended so we planned to go see him. Someone had told me about this tailor and when Jintana and I went on a cruise I went to him and had a suit made in case there was any reason to dress up on the ship. He made a beautiful suit and it turned out I didn't need it. So now I have the suit in my closet and the chances of wearing it in Thailand are zero.

The cruise? I'm glad you asked. I'd wanted Jintana to see what my life had been like on the ships so last year we booked a cruise out of Hong Kong to Japan and back. I had some trepidation, as the cruises I had worked were filled with conservative American passengers and I was afraid they'd all gone Trump and we'd face racist comments. As with 90% of my worries, it was silly because the ship was filled with Chinese people out of Hong Kong. Jintana felt they looked down on her because they thought she was a gold digger taking advantage of an old man. It's hard to tell 3000 people she worked at a university for 26 years, owns her own house, and was doing just fine before I came along. Ah, humans.

I loved being back on the ocean but the ship was huge and felt wrong to me. There was a feeling of being hustled, which is true of all cheaper cruises where they have to make up for the low fares by making money on board. It was understandable and I knew it would happen but it was still uncomfortable.

The other problem is Jintana gets motion sickness and the last two nights the ship rocked a bit. She wasn't sick but she wasn't happy either. All in all, it was a mixed bag. I'd like to take the kids on a cruise, but I'm not sure that's in the cards. No big deal, as I had twenty years of seeing the world on ships.

Back to the Walking Street, where I had to search awhile to find a trash bin for my corn cob. I didn't buy anything. After awhile I walked back to the car and stopped at Annie's Place where they have the open mic every Sunday night. I thought again about going, but the parking is awful and the setup not that great. I think it's more of a rock 'n roll situation and that is definitely out of my league. Noisy bar, drunk crowds, equals a bad night for me.

There were some comedians who could open for rock bands and they have my total admiration. That is a skill on a whole other level.

Wow, just had a memory of opening for Donna Summers in Atlantic City. She was a disco queen and if anything was the opposite of disco it was me. It was like having Bob Newhart open for Megadeth. I struggled mightily and got them with some druggie jokes at the end, but it was not a glorious experience. To show you how long ago that was, this was the first casino to open in Atlantic City and it was gangbusters. People were lined up around the block to play blackjack at

Mike Neun

tables with a 25 dollar minimum. Big bucks in those days.

Later I opened for Mel Tillis at Harrah's in Atlantic City and when I got there one of the stagehands warned me that the sound was weird and I wouldn't hear the audience. Every comedian who worked there thought they were bombing, but they weren't. They just couldn't hear the laughs. Luckily I'd played a couple of fairgrounds and could adjust.

Mel Tillis was a country singer famous for his stuttering problem. When he sang you wouldn't know it, but when he talked he stuttered and he made light of it. Like all country acts he had a tour bus, and on the side was painted M-m-m-m-Mel T-t-t-t-Tillis. I loved that. I usually hung out with the musicians and roadies and I got to know the driver of the bus, who was a good guy. One day I walked out of the casino and he was there with the bus.

"Where are you going?" he asked.

"To the drugstore. I need toothpaste."

"Hop in," he said, "I'll take you."

Weird. Riding a luxury tour bus three blocks to buy toothpaste. Life is fun.

I liked country acts and opened for a bunch of them. They all seemed down to earth and most of them had played a lot of tough bars before they hit the big time. We're talking bars with chicken wire in front of the stage so they wouldn't get hit by flying beer bottles. I'd forgotten how many country people I'd worked with but now their names come back to me, Crystal Gayle, Loretta Lynn, Mickey Gilley, Ronnie Milsap, Ray Stevens, Mel Tillis...I'm sure there were more and I'm sure I'll think of them at 4 a.m. tonight. That's how my memory works. All of them were good to work with.

The best opening act line I ever heard was Jerry Van Dyke walking on stage and saying, "I can't tell you how happy I am to be in front of a thousand people who came to see someone else."

This morning I had breakfast with Jintana and Kadjang and then took another walk through town. I have to do this more often. I love walking and exploring places and Chiangmai is both lively and ever-changing. I remember long ago going back to see my brother in Eugene, Oregon, and walking around downtown thinking it was incredibly boring. No street vendors, no tuk tuks, no pedicabs, no sidewalk restaurants and cafes. Nobody was walking! Another time Jintana and I went to a mall in the states and it felt like a mausoleum. Thai malls always have shows going on with loudspeakers blaring and lots of people because on a summer day in Thailand everyone flocks to anyplace that's air-conditioned. Thai malls are alive. U.S. malls are dying.

So I walked around town and saw a bookstore. I love bookstores but it's been a long time since I've been in one. The bridge club has a library where people trade books for free, and when I drive I listen to audio books instead of music. Music was my job, books are my life. At the moment I'm re-listening to Ron Chernow's book about Ulysses S. Grant because I'm playing golf with Joe, a southerner steeped in Robert E. Lee and Louisiana history. He thinks Grant was a drunk and a scoundrel and I couldn't remember the stuff I'd read three years ago. Knowledge is power and I know he'll be delighted to have me enlighten him.

Did you know Grant was a consummate horseman? As a kid he would train horses no one could handle and at West Point he dazzled his graduation classmates by jumping a horse over a high bar and that record stood for years.

I first listened to the Grant book when I drove out to Chiangmai Highlands. I played golf there for 15 years and it's a 45-minute drive each way. I listened to a lot of books. Hell, I listened to *War and Peace*! It took a month, and as Woody Allen said, "It's about Russia."

Mike Neun

Between that and the Grant biography I have reaffirmed my idea that all war is incredibly sad, with millions of young people losing their lives because old people are too arrogant or stupid to figure things out. War is the worst form of insanity and for every brilliant commander there are twenty who throw their troops into hopeless situations. Fuck war.

You see how books can get you riled up? Maybe that's why I used to get angry on the golf course. I was pissed off at Napoleon. How stupid do you have to be to march into Russia in the wintertime? Sure, and after that we can attack Saudi Arabia in July! Good plan!

You see what kind of thoughts come from walking around Chiangmai? The only downside was that I'd already had two cups of coffee, for there were great little coffee places everywhere I looked. I think I should organize coffee tours of Chiangmai. We'd just walk from place to place, sampling coffee on every block.

The bars have changed. When I first got here Loi Kroh street was filled with loud bars filled with heavily made up bargirls in short skirts and halter tops. Now the mayor has tried to clean up the town and there are far fewer girly bars. There used to be a bar by the moat called the Spotlight and I remember a friend taking me there. There were lots of girls on stage pole dancing and I remember looking in the mirror behind the bar and thinking, "Look at those old guys, staring at those young girls." Then I realized I was one of those old guys.

I remember a drunken white college girl getting up on stage with the Thai pole dancers and taking off her clothes while her friends cheered. And I thought, tomorrow she gets to go back to her normal life. Tomorrow, those Thai girls will be back on that stage.

And now a word about Thai massage. It is one of the reasons I moved here. A good Thai massage is the most heavenly thing I have ever experienced. You go in, take off your clothes and put on pajamas, taking a while to figure out how to tie the drawstring on the pants. Then you lie down on your back and the masseuse comes in, places her/his hands together in a wai, and then starts with your feet. You are on a mattress on the floor so the masseuse can use the leverage of their entire body to lean into you. Some of them are incredibly strong and don't know it, so you have to ask them to ease up. The Thai word for *softer* is *bow bow* and I learned that in a hurry.

They massage your entire body, bending limbs in ways you never thought possible and in time it will be like a meditation where your thoughts fade away and you fall into a state of peace. Halfway through they have you roll onto your stomach and start with the feet again, working up through your body. Finally, they sit behind you, cross their legs and you rest your head on a pillow in their lap while they do more on your neck and head. Then they sit you up and stretch your arms and neck and then with a few cupped hands taps to the back you are done. It is the absolute best my body has ever felt. Two hours of magic.

There are all kinds of massages. Oil, hot stones, foot massage, head and shoulder massage, and so on. They are all good. You can't go wrong.

And yes, you can get *happy ending* massages. In fifteen years I've been offered them twice and both times they caught me by surprise. I declined.

You see? Walking around Chiangmai brings back all kinds of memories.

Mike Neun

GOOD GUY, BAD GUY, WHO KNOWS?

I think previously I said something about trying to be a good person. The truth is there were times when I wasn't and those memories kept me up at night for years. Mostly they were times when I was a coward, when I didn't do the right thing. I can handle adversity and come back but I really can't handle situations when I should've stepped up and didn't. So no, I wasn't always a good person. I let people down, I failed to stand up to bullies, and those things haunt me on those late nights when I'm wide awake for no reason.

I thought about that a lot and I am thankful I never had enough power to make huge mistakes. Normal people can only hurt one or two people at a time. Powerful people can hurt millions. How do they sleep at night?

If you haven't been a good person the Golf Gods may wait years but sooner or later they'll punish you. This morning I played the worst game of golf I've played in five years. Just dreadful. The good news is I didn't throw any clubs and apologized to my caddy while I was swearing at myself. I think she understood.

There's a bar in town, Boy Blue's Bar, owned by a fine Thai blues and rock guitar player named Boy Blue. On Sundays they have an open mic and the first time I played it I just killed. I asked if I could just do one song, and he said sure. When my turn came I started to walk up with my Martin D-41 12-string guitar and his eyes lit up. The other musicians were dazzled by it too and I realized I'd played it for 30 years and hadn't thought much about it. After I did my set a guy said I should be careful because someone might try to steal it. I don't know how much it's worth, because the neck is broken above the nut. The airlines did it.

In the old days you could carry a guitar on a plane. After 9/11 you had to check it in as baggage. Not only that, you had to sign a waver saying it was improperly packed. You could have it in a bullet proof Kevlar case wrapped in bubble wrap and they'll still say it's improperly packed, which means that when (not if, when) they break it they won't pay for it. I always signed that waver Mickey Mouse and nobody noticed.

The airlines broke my guitar about once every two years and my all-time hero is the guy who wrote the song about United Airlines breaking his guitar. It went viral and was sweet revenge for all of us powerless guitar players.

The last time they broke it I was flying to a ship to do shows and you'd be amazed how few guitar repair shops there are on cruise ships. I went down to the carpenter shop in crew area and they found some Elmer's Glue. Amazingly, I'd toured the Martin factory in Nazareth, PA, and they told me after experimenting with hundreds of glues, Elmer's had turned out to be the best and was the glue they used for their guitars. So I got lucky on the ship. I glued the peg head back to the neck, thankful it had broken with jagged edges so there was a lot of glue area.

I didn't have clamps and knew the glue wouldn't take the strain so I resorted to my golf knowledge. Years ago

Mike Neun

when I was a kid working in the pro shop, the clubheads for drivers and fairway woods were made of persimmon and the shaft was stuck through the head. Then it was "whipped." Whipping is twine, like fishing line, wrapped around the head where it meets the shaft and it's amazingly strong. So I got some dark blue line and whipped my guitar peg head to the neck. It held, and I did my shows.

That whipping has held for 20 years. So I play a broken guitar.

The guitar has had a couple other adventures. Once the airlines lost it and promised to deliver it to my house. On the day of the delivery I called and they said yes, they'd delivered it. Well, it hadn't come to me so I went next door to see if they'd heard anything and there, inside the screen door, was my guitar. I love the airlines.

Another time I flew to Costa Rica and they lost my guitar. I went through the usual routine, checking with the baggage people and putting in a claim and then there was nothing to do but go to the ship. It was a long drive in a minivan. Luckily the ship was there overnight so the next morning I got the ship's agent to drive me back to the airport. I walked in and went to the baggage area to ask the people about my guitar. I looked over and there, circling alone on the conveyor belt where anyone could pick it up, was my guitar.

Now it sits in the corner and I haven't picked it up in three months. I played that Boy Blues open mic and it was perfect. There was a table of young people in front and while Boy was setting up the mics I said to them, "I bet you're so excited to hear a really old guy play." They laughed. I did the country song and it went over really well. Boy came up smiling and asked if I could do another so I did my love song, "I'm in Love with Me", and people loved that too. Lots of applause. Perfect. I walked off thinking I'd found a home, a place to play in Chiangmai.

I figured I'd go back to Boy's every week and build up a following but it didn't work. I sang other comedy songs and they fell flat. Also, the crowd was getting louder and more rock and roll. The last couple of times weren't good at all. I realized my bar career in Chiangmai was over and that pretty much means my career on stage was over. That's okay. I tried coming up with new material and it didn't happen so I'm content in the thought that I had my beautiful show biz moments and I really do like my quiet life with Jintana and her family. I wouldn't have it any other way.

Mike Neun

PEOPLE KEEP SURPRISING ME

I never planned to be a comedian, it just happened. My whole life was random and my friends were too. In college I majored in journalism and was sports editor of the University of Washington Daily. We had a photographer named Bob Peterson, who was the son of the trainer of the football team. Bob was a big guy, always cheerful, and my lasting memory is of him dancing on my desk for no reason. I just thought of him as another bumbling student like the rest of us. Wrong.

Bob became one of the great photographers in the U.S., with pictures and cover shots in Sports Illustrated, Life, and the other big magazines of the time. He came up with iconic photographs of presidents, sports heroes, movie stars, authors—in short, the biggest names of our times. He also did some of the most iconic Nike ads with famous athletes.

Bob put out a coffee table book recently of his favorite photos, with his picture of Clint Eastwood as Dirty Harry on the cover. I have it in front of me and can't believe I know someone who did all that.

To put it in perspective, he also did a lot of my head shots and he also has a video tape of the dreaded Carson show where I bombed in front of millions of viewers. I have never seen it, and never will.

From Bob's wife, Lynn:

> *I was telling my sister about it (this book) last night and remembered the time you and Brian arrived in our apartment in NY on a Sunday morning when we were out of town and my parents and another couple were having breakfast having spent the night before— big surprise for all of you and then you entertained them for an hour and they were thrilled!*

Paul West was part of our Seattle group too. I first got to know him when he was playing the piano bar with Lee Westwood on bass at the Hungry Turtle down on Lake Union. Paul was a fine jazz piano player and singer who could also belt out the Flanders and Swan masterpiece, "Have Some Madeira My Dear." When I was struggling between jobs, I would go see Paul and he'd have me do some comedy songs. I knew him as a piano player in a bar. Wrong again.

Paul went down to L.A. to do voice overs and then got hired by Microsoft in their marketing department. Next thing I knew he was a millionaire. But he still played piano gigs around town and his ultimate dream was to go play piano at a bistro in Paris.

Paul West died awhile ago and we lost one of the most up-beat and talented people I've ever known.

Mike Channing is a salmon fisherman who lives with his wife, Jenny, in Indianola, outside of Seattle. He's also a fine writer, poet, guitar player and one of my all-time closest friends. He and my brother are the two best email writers I have ever known and we also did a lot of sailing together. Everything I've ever known about tossing fish I learned from him. He never became rich or famous but he is a life-long friend and someone I really respect. I wish he'd move to Chiangmai but the salmon fishing here is not that good.

Mike Neun

Derek Schade was the golf pro at Highlands when I first started playing there and our friendship has lasted. He's a Canadian hockey player (all Canadian boys were hockey players apparently) who switched to golf and came to Thailand to work on his game before trying for the tour. His tour dreams didn't work out but he got hired by a golf management company and that evolved into his job at Chiangmai Highlands. He's a fine golfer and great guy and in the early years we wrote a book together about golf and life in Thailand. When we finished we had mixed feelings about publishing it. One, it would be a lot of work and two, we weren't sure we wanted a our Bangkok stories to get out, even though they weren't that scandalous. That book languishes in our computers.

Derek plays left-handed and I can't remember him ever taking a practice swing. He just walks up and hits the ball, usually a long way with a little fade. Hank Haney, the pro who coached Tiger Woods, once came to Thailand to do some promotions and he gave a presentation at Derek's course. He tried to get Derek to switch to playing a draw, but that didn't take.

Derek worked at Highlands but then got offered a general manager job at Lotus Valley in Bangkok. Now he's back down there with his wife, Nok, and their two small children. We've played tons of golf together, spent hours talking about golf and life, and drunk way too much in bad bars. We've made lots of people happy in those bars because we have the same philosophy. We figure it's our job to give the people who work there one good night and some relief from dealing with drunken jerks. We laughed, bought drinks and wildly overtipped everyone, including people mopping floors.

Oh yes, we always took a car and driver, because we are not totally stupid.

Derek is really good at his job.

This story broke me up. One of the big problems on a crowded course is slow play and Derek and the caddies came up with a brilliant plan. When a group was holding up the course, Derek would go out but he wouldn't even talk to the golfers. He would start yelling at the caddies. The caddies were in on it and would try to look contrite as he berated them for letting their group fall so far behind. This wasn't easy, because they were trying not to laugh. The golfers would feel sorry for the caddies and speed up. Genius!

He's one of the best people I've met here and it's not because he gets a lot of free golf shirts and gives me some whenever I go visit, although that's a huge point in his favor.

Doug Moeller was a guy I knew in college and he was kind of a party animal. I worried about him. Would he make it in the real world? We skied a lot together and after college he talked me into flying to Germany, renting a VW Beetle and cruising through Europe.

I think we were the only people crazy enough to go to Octoberfest in Munich without bothering to book a place to stay. Doug solved it by talking a couple of girls into letting us sleep on their floor.

In Zermat, Switzerland, we wanted to ski on the glacier but didn't have enough money for the tram. Doug began talking to a group of Polish students and soon we'd formed the International Student's Society and got a group rate. It was a learning experience for me as I'd grown up in Detroit where people told Polish jokes and made fun of Hungarians, Italians, Chinese, and every other minority. Yes, equal opportunity racists. That day on the mountain those students were bright, handsome people and way more sophisticated than we were. Image shattered.

Mike Neun

Later on he got a job in the real estate division at McDonalds and every new employee has to work one of the restaurants for two weeks so they'll know the basic business. We spread out and searched Seattle, hoping to find him in his little hat flipping burgers but somehow he eluded us. I'd see him now and then when I got back to Seattle and assumed he was just a guy with a job, but then he got transferred to Hong Kong to handle all the real estate deals for McDonald's in mainland China. Yes, there was the guy I worried about, living in a luxury apartment on Victoria Peak, making a huge amount of money and dealing with the top brass all over China.

Doug married a beautiful Chinese doctor and he's happily retired while she has a top job in medical insurance. So the party animal came out way more prosperous than any of us.

Just for the record, when I lived in Monterey I went to the Folk Festival and Bob Dylan did a set. I predicted he'd never make the big time. I'm right on top of this stuff.

THE VIRUS AND ME

It's quiet here in Chiangmai. We haven't been as hard hit as other countries, so far but summer schools are closed, the tourist industry is shattered, and lots of people are staying home. The Bridge Club of Chiangmai will probably close for awhile, and that seems smart. If you have 40 or 50 of the most vulnerable people passing cards from table to table I would guess viruses would be lined up trying to get in.

Our family is doing fine. Jintana, Tai and the kids went to Central Festival Mall yesterday and had a good time. I played golf this morning with Ploy, my caddy, and we had a pleasant round.

There is no run on toilet paper. The stores and restaurants are open. Jintana and Tai are still working. People are calm. My vast stock portfolio (I use "vast" to mean it could last another year or two) has taken a hit. I'm happy to be here in Thailand and willing to accept whatever happens to me. I had a great life and am way ahead of the game. I worry for the kids, and will do whatever it takes to help them. To all my friends from over the years, I wish you the best and thank you. It's been a great ride.

Mike Neun, March 23, 2020

The End

Made in the USA
Monee, IL
05 May 2021